ADVANCE PRAISE FOR *YOUR FINEST WORK*

"If you are searching for deep wisdom and practical steps to navigate a mid-career shift, this is a brilliant read. Identify traps you may be unintentionally setting that keep you stuck. If you yearn for more in a world that can be noisy and overwhelming, grab this book and clear the clutter. Put yourself in charge of your career and your life."

—**HELEN HORYZA**, ACC, author of *Elevate Your Career: Live a Life You're Truly Proud Of*

"*Your Finest Work* is filled with pragmatic advice for becoming a more effective leader. One of Merideth's strengths is helping leaders see different perspectives and use that awareness to create mutually beneficial outcomes. The strategies I have learned from Merideth have helped me refine my own leadership, as well as given me tools to share with others to help them grow."

—**KEIA COLE**, Chief Digital Officer, Brooklyn Sports & Entertainment Global

"Like most meaningful things in life, there is no guidebook on how to create and prosper in a fulfilling career. *Your Finest Work* helps you make your own guidebook to find your own North Star and implement a...deliberate career path. Without this support, a career can be subject to the winds of chance or can be stuck...for years. With direction from *Your Finest Work*, you can take control of your own career, directing it towards a meaningful future."

—**NOAH GOLDSTEIN**, PhD, leading Fortune 100 companies toward carbon and climate resilience

"This remarkable book could not be more timely....Merideth Mehlberg offers an insightful and practical path to achievable career and life transformation. Through relatable and engaging stories, she inspires all of us to step forward with intention in finding our finest work."

—**CARISUE BENCH**, Human Capital Strategist and Coach

"There are books on theory and then there are books where it's clear the author has truly been in the trenches and they can make their theories actionable. Merideth accomplishes the latter with *Your Finest Work*. She demonstrates that she's been there with her clients and cares deeply about providing you (the reader) with clear, actionable steps to make work work for you. Let this book be your guide out of the traps you're barely conscious of and into a satisfying career path, no matter where you are now."

—**LAURA BERMAN FORTGANG**, MCC, author of *Now What?® 90 Days to a New Life Direction* and *Living Your Best Life*

"The world is changing faster than ever. With shifts in AI, politics, global health and climate, it might feel like nothing we do matters and sticks. *Your Finest Work* cuts through all the chaos and helps you focus on what matters the most to professionals—having a dream career. Merideth shows you the tools and gives you a step-by-step guide to transform your life and achieve that dream."

—**JIA JIANG**, award-winning author, speaker, and owner of Rejection Therapy

"Merideth provides you with practical tools to navigate the most pivotal moments in your career. Her insightful and thoughtful questions and anecdotes throughout the book help you to explore exactly what motivates you and discover what will bring you fulfillment and joy in the next phase of your career. Without Merideth's keen assistance, I doubt I would have landed where I find myself today—in a new and exciting moment in my professional life."

—**JESSICA GOLDSTEIN**, Senior Director, NPR Events and Experiential Programming

"In the 20 years I've known Mer, I've observed her excellence as a teammate, a leader, and a coach. She has taught many, including me, lessons on leadership and growth using a style that injects equal doses of candor, compassion, and optimism. This book has distilled that wisdom into a practical framework that made me want to listen to her advice once more."

—**PETER WEIS**, Supply Chain Executive and CIO, teacher, speaker, and digital transformation expert

"Merideth does a masterful job of connecting the dots for how to have your career truly work for you. The stories of real leaders making shifts of their own make this book enjoyable to read and the lessons easy to grasp. Read *Your Finest Work* and change your life for the better, starting today."

—**ALLISON MASLAN**, author of *Scale or Fail*

"Modern leadership requires us to be both attuned to what we ourselves need as individuals and to those around us and what they need from us as leaders. Supporting our teams and growing our careers go in tandem.... The stories in *Your Finest Work* help connect our real-life experiences to opportunities we have to move forward both our leadership and the world we want to shape."

—**ELENE TERRY**, modern leader of innovative silicon and system products

"Merideth Mehlberg is an amazing listener, a thoughtful coach, and a great human with a lot of experience navigating around tricky career situations. She brings a level of honesty and authenticity to every interaction, which makes partnering with her a real joy. I...am excited for the world to get a part of her thoughtful playbook through this book."

—**DINI MEHTA**, CRO, investor and board member

"I'll admit that initially I was interested in providing *Your Finest Work* as a resource to share with others. However, when I started to read it, I was so inspired...that I couldn't put it down; and I've already noted multiple lessons to apply to my own life. This book is easy to read and provides both inspiration and structure to support you in putting it into action....I will now be recommending this book to many!"

—**NICOLA RIES TAGGART**, author of *Calm the Chaos Journal* and *Calm the Chaos Cards*

"In *Your Finest Work*, Merideth Mehlberg presents a transformative blueprint that empowers readers to rise above the noise and find purpose in their careers. Whether you are a seasoned executive or a recent graduate, this book will revolutionize the way you approach your professional journey."

—**MIKE VARDY**, Productivity Expert, creator of TimeCrafting

"In her book, *Your Finest Work*, Merideth Mehlberg has accomplished what many books in this category fail to do. She has given the reader a clear path to fulfillment in their career and personal life. She does this through thoughtful questions and coaching examples that allow us to grab the reins of our life and see ourselves as the architects of our life experiences…. In this book, Merideth makes it possible for the reader to do the work to reclaim their sense of agency. Thank you for this gift."

—**MARIA NEMETH**, PhD, MCC, Director, Academy for Coaching Excellence, author of *The Energy of Money*

"If you are looking to get to know yourself better, to claim your inner hopes and dreams, and live authentically the best life you can, read *Your Finest Work*. My one-on-one coaching with Merideth has been nothing short of profound. Yes, I advanced my career, my salary, and my title, but it's the personal growth that's made all the difference. Merideth helped me expand my vision of who I am and how I can be. How wonderful that the framework I used to live up to the potential of who I am at my best is now available here."

—**ALISSA REITER**, CMO, Coach and Advisor

"Too many people feel cautious about AI and the disruption it brings. If you count yourself as one of them, follow the strategies in this book to ground yourself. *Your Finest Work* offers a structured approach to taking your seat at the leadership table while remaining true to your values. You have a role to play as a writer of the future, shaping the world with better outcomes for all."

—**ASHA KEDDY**, Senior Executive and Technology Futurist, leading end-to-end innovation and monetization of current and new markets

YOUR
FINEST
WORK

YOUR FINEST WORK

CAREER FULFILLMENT IN A COMPLICATED WORLD

MERIDETH MEHLBERG
MASTER COACH AND CAREER STRATEGIST

Lively **hood**
PRESS

Contact the publisher at www.meridethmehlberg.com

Want to buy a lot of these books? Wonderful. We can help. We can also customize and co-brand Your Finest Work. Please contact us at info@yourfinestwork.com for more info.

Design by Vanessa Mendozzi

Publisher's Cataloging-in-Publication Data
Names: Mehlberg, Merideth, author.
Title: Your finest work: career fulfillment in a complicated world / Merideth Mehlberg.
Description: Alameda, CA: Livelyhood Press, 2023.
Identifiers: ISBN 979-8-9891573-0-3 (paperback) | ISBN 979-8-9891573-1-0 (ebook)
Subjects: LCSH: Success in business. | Executive ability. | Leadership. | Career development. | Vocational guidance. | Job satisfaction. | BISAC: BUSINESS & ECONOMICS / Leadership. | SELF-HELP / Personal Growth / Success.
Classification: LCC HF5549.5.J63 M44 2023 (print) | LCC HF5549.5.J63 (ebook) | DDC 650.1--dc23.

LCCN: 2023919366

DISCLAIMER
This book contains real stories about real people. All stories have been shared with permission, with identifying information changed to protect confidentiality. This book is about coaching and is not intended as a substitute for professional legal, financial, medical, or psychotherapeutic advice.

Livelyhood Press
1516 Oak St. Suite 328
Alameda, CA 94501

*For Chris Bailey and all the amazing leaders
I've had the privilege to coach to their finest work.*

BONUS MATERIALS

Reading this book is an important first step to accessing your finest work. It is an excellent companion to what career fulfillment truly requires: self-reflection and action. To help you get started with both, I've created some free tools you can download, including:

A Self-Assessment Quiz and Results Key – In just a few minutes, confirm the areas that most need your attention to increase your professional satisfaction, impact, and success.

A Quick Action Guide – Quickly focus your attention on some professional practices and tactics that can help you close the gap between where you are now and where you want to be.

Download these and other bonus materials at **www.yourfinestwork.com**

CONTENTS

FOREWORD

This is a very timely book. It is perhaps the best book I have read for course correcting one's work in the 2020s. If you are looking for a book to help you construct a better resume or to interview better, look elsewhere. This book will force you to get to your truth, your vision, and your passion, allowing you to course-correct as you progress along your chosen work path.

"Career" increasingly seems to be a word of the 20th century. Post-WWII, the workplace based upon the Industrial Age model of the factory and hierarchical corporations is something that has faded away. Pay your dues, move around a lot, impress the boss, master corporate politics, compete with your fellow managers, stay with a company for decades and end up with the gold watch feels as archaic as the landline phone.

Career now means coming from where you are to get to who you are, what you love, and what you are good at doing. This book will help you on this journey.

Each chapter provides a lesson, a chunk of truth. Merideth does this by profiling some of her many clients to represent various places where people get stuck. I am sure that you will find you can relate to many of these anecdotes and derive benefit from the clients' journeys. Merideth has clearly curated the most instructive case studies for you. Anyone starting out on their work journey or anyone needing a course correction in mid-life will derive great benefit from reading this book.

As a futurist and speaker, I have met Merideth several times, as she was part of an elite group of executive coaches that kept inviting me back to speak to them. I always enjoy speaking to the "best of the best" in any human endeavor as I know they will benefit most from being challenged to think openly about the future, which they regard as their turf. In my recent interactions with her, I have been impressed with her insights and wisdom. As a reader you will be impressed as well.

If you know of my work, you know that I coined the phrase "The Shift Age," which is the age we are now in. We are in a time of historic shift, where what was is rapidly receding and what will be is rushing in. I am in the midst of writing a series of books about the 2020s, which is the most disruptive decade in human history. In a time of such disruption and transformation there is no going back, only forward. The speed of change is accelerating. This means that even those who think clearly and have taken correct, intuitive steps to move forward may, in time, find the need to adapt and alter direction. One would have to be brain dead to believe that one knows where humanity is going, where business is going, or where professions are going.

Increasingly it is self-knowledge and clarity that will benefit the employee, manager, director, or leader of any effort or entity. Merideth helps the reader gain insight into both the self and the market. In these times, both are needed. I can only imagine the gratitude that flows back to her from her clients. They are lucky to have retained her as a coach. Reading this book is the next best thing. Enjoy and benefit from this book. I am confident you will.

David Houle

FUTURIST | JULY 2023

PREFACE

Life today is in many ways far different than it was just a few years ago. The pandemic, political polarization, wars, gun violence, systemic racism, inflation, rapid technological change, and the urgency of the climate crisis are sources of worry for us all. We confront problems that range from how to raise our children to how to run our companies. We want to protect our kids, our jobs, and our way of life. More than ever we want to make our work fulfilling and count for something in the world. But many of us are unsure how to go about this.

The complexities of our time and the scramble to come to terms with them are almost overwhelming. Anywhere we look we see strife and struggle—in our personal lives, our work lives, our communities, and throughout the world.

Relatively few people experience flow—or even engagement—in their work these days. Some of us were raised to believe that good work speaks for itself, creating fulfillment and happiness in our careers and our lives. Others embarked on a career expecting to find their true calling in life. The reality is that many of us have reached mid-career and find our work life is something we hadn't anticipated and don't care to continue. Some people confess to feeling dead inside from the compromises and disappointments in their work life.

Even if you are one of the fortunate few who enjoy the

work they do, you may still feel you've failed to realize your full potential and wonder if you should be thinking about and doing bigger things. Whether your ambition is to reach the top of the career ladder or simply to do work that makes a real difference in these troubled times, you may long for change but feel unsure how to proceed.

You may feel paralyzed by the prospect of making any kind of career shift, whether to a new line of work, a new job, or even just growing in your current situation. The requirements and constraints seem too great, and so you remain stuck in place.

If you have been focused, head down in your job, and suddenly look up to find yourself either laid off or behind where your colleagues are, you may feel at sea when it comes to securing new employment or catching up with those ahead of you. You may have no network or structure you can turn to for help. Or if you are one of the lucky ones still employed after a reduction in force, you may find you and your teammates inundated with work you've inherited from others.

You may feel frustrated by feedback you've received about your performance or overlooked despite your considerable experience and qualifications. As a result, you may react negatively to constructive criticism while at the same time recognizing that it contains at least a kernel of truth.

Whether you never identified a good fit for your talents and interests or were influenced early in life by people around you to become something that you didn't really want to be or have grown out of, you may feel uncertain about your next steps. You may have doubts about whether you can truly spread your wings and fly.

If you see yourself in any one of these situations, then this book is for you. I have been an executive coach and career strategist since the early 2000s. I began my career as a recruiter for the global staffing company Adecco, where I became an expert translator between two audiences: employees and employers. Later, I advanced up the ranks of leadership in product management at Adecco and at two different startups, delivering strategic solutions designed to resolve thorny customer challenges. As a coach with such a pragmatic background, I am able to cut through complexity and see success patterns to guide my executive clients into more of what they want, and less of what they don't. A U.C. Berkeley graduate and Master Certified Coach (MCC), I've worked with emerging and established executives in Fortune 100 companies, startups, and nonprofits across many industries to transform careers and lives. In this book I've taken what I've learned on my journey and crystallized it into an easy-to-read primer that will help you realize your full potential and do your finest work.

INTRODUCTION

I sensed Kelly's impatience the minute our consultation began. A senior leader in job transition, she was looking for help with her job search. She blurted out that her last two jobs had not been good fits, with her bosses not meshing well with her direct, tell-it-like-it-is style. As she talked, I tried to grasp whether her intention was a true career move or simply landing another job. I asked her to describe her dream role. As expected, her vision was short on details and painted a fuzzy, indistinct picture.

As she talked, Kelly stated more than once that she was an impatient person; she wanted to know how quickly we would get to updating her resume and practicing interviewing. After a few minutes, I stopped the conversation and announced that I was not the coach for her. Given her stated goals, working together would not bring out my best and so was not a good investment for her.

She was shocked and asked me why.

"My interest and specialty is in helping people slow down and take some time for career design, rather than jumping right into the job search. I don't sense that you are open to that approach right now," I said.

After a bit, she agreed with me. I gave her a referral to a resume writer, and she moved on with her job search.

In my view, Kelly's opportunity at this juncture was multi-dimensional:

- to clarify what had not worked for her in her past experiences
- to take responsibility for her part in perpetuating what was not working for her in these roles and take steps to remedy the issues so they didn't happen again
- to design her future career steps to make sure that she would feel supported, could thrive, and would be fulfilled

At this point in her life, this type of deeper career inquiry did not register with Kelly and was not of interest. She was not willing to slow down her thinking enough to ponder and strategize about how to resolve these issues. I would not be surprised to learn if, in her next role, she found herself in a similar situation to what she had experienced in the past: dissatisfied and misunderstood.

THE OPPORTUNITY

We are living through an unprecedented time in human history. According to futurists—including my favorite, David Houle—we are experiencing a fundamental rewiring of what it means to be human, including how we live and work in the world. This experience is taking an undeniable toll on all of us and on all facets of our lives, including our careers.

At work we are rewarded for making quick decisions within set constraints. The reactive nature of life in general can make it challenging for us to indulge in the blue-sky thinking that intentional career design requires. As a result, we often have blinders on and are shaped solely by our experiences to date. Our personal history colors our perception of what is possible. We are not accustomed to giving ourselves room in our careers to explore what it truly means to be alive and the direction we want to move in the future. But that is what's necessary if we are to realize our full potential and do our finest work.

As an executive coach, in any given week I'm involved in about thirty conversations concerning how leaders are navigating their careers during these turbulent times. Whether I'm facilitating cohorts of senior executives or conducting one-on-one coaching sessions, my ongoing theme is how professionals surrounded by disruptive change can keep their own best interests and career fulfillment to the forefront, while also doing the best work of their lives for their organizations, communities, and families.

In many of these conversations, I hear one or more variations on the following themes:

- feeling overlooked, undervalued, misunderstood, and frustrated (like Kelly)
- not knowing what they want, but certain it's different from what they have
- vacillating between whether to stay in their job or leave
- feeling exhausted, beyond stressed, and not able to take much more
- wanting their good work to speak for itself and open doors—and being disappointed when it doesn't
- resisting asking for help, fearing it may make them look weak or be an imposition on others
- dreading the idea of having to network, job search, or start over

- paralyzed about making a mistake—wanting to "do things right"
- perhaps most often, feeling unsure about where to start to make a difference in their situation

Gallup's annual employee engagement survey consistently reports that many people are disengaged from their careers. The 2021 poll revealed that just 36 percent of American workers remain engaged in their jobs. That means almost two-thirds are disengaged. Globally the 2021 percentage of disengaged workers was even higher, approaching 80 percent. These numbers have grown over time, beginning pre-pandemic.

The statistics speak for themselves—many professionals are suffering through their workdays, operating at less than their full capacity and capability. Many feel disconnected from their workplace, from what they value, and what they want professionally.

Instead of feeling demoralized by these statistics, I pay attention to the 36 percent who remain engaged at work. What can we learn from them? I have made it my life's work to study these folks, looking into what is different about their approach. I've learned that engaged professionals operate in a way that moves them ever closer to the work-life experience they desire. They start, as you must, with a simple but powerful realization: you alone are in the driver's seat. Especially now, when the world is so disrupted, you can't afford to be asleep at the wheel. When you take charge of your career, you can leverage your talents to enjoy career fulfillment, impact, and success while meeting the complex challenges we face in our companies and communities. To do both, you need to be at your finest. Your family, your colleagues, your company, your community, and yes, even the world, needs you at your best.

The benefits of following a discerning career path are many. They include landing the job you want, getting a promotion to the next level, or making a strong start down a new career path. But it's more than these things. The intangible benefits can include building rich relationships with others, defining your own personal version of success, coming back to life after a setback, and aligning your work with your perceived purpose in life. Above all, it means taking charge of your life to the greatest possible extent, rather than being controlled by other people or events.

If you have experienced a wake-up call and long to move from being disengaged to fully engaged, to doing your finest work, there is a clear roadmap, which I lay out in this book. Chapters 2–8 discuss seven major traps that prevent us from reaching the goal and the strategies, practices, and tactics that will allow you to avoid or defeat these traps.

To summarize:

YOU SUFFER WHEN YOU:	YOU THRIVE WHEN YOU:
Are asleep at the wheel	Become an intentional architect
Focus on everyone else's agenda	Define your North Star
Run on empty	Fill your tank
Fixate on doing things right	Take imperfect action
Have a transactional focus	Fine-tune your powers of perception
Try to do it all yourself	Broaden your base of support
Don't tell a compelling career story	Sharpen your professional narrative

Success comes from taking targeted action to reduce your suffering and increase your ability to thrive. To pinpoint where best to focus your attention, I've created a Self-Assessment Quiz and Results Key for you as a complement to this book. You can access this, as well as other free tools at **www.yourfinestwork.com**.

The playbook to experience your finest work is in your hands. It starts with your wake-up call.

1. THE WAKE-UP CALL

The Opening You Need to Transform Your Career

I was thirty-five years old. I hadn't thought my adult life would be like this. As I sat at my desk and took another sip of lukewarm coffee, I could feel the stress rising in my chest while I examined my schedule for the day. As a product line manager for a supply chain software startup, eight straight hours of meetings was my norm; this day would be no exception. The team of software developers, quality assurance professionals, and product managers I co-directed was waiting on me for the remaining requirements for the current software build. Everyone needed something from me to keep moving and unblock obstacles. Behind schedule and with senior leadership breathing down our necks, we felt demoralized by the prospect of our planned scope falling short of customer expectations. However, we were doing everything we could, given the strict schedule and the budget constraints placed on us from above.

Feeling like I was participating in an exercise in futility, I soldiered on in service of the team that mastered herculean tasks daily. Vaguely aware that this job was not working for me, I hunkered down for yet another marathon workday in my cubicle.

Later that week I was sitting in my acupuncturist's office; I had turned to acupuncture after Western medical science failed me. I was waiting to hear the results of a battery of tests she'd ordered. Five years into my quest to have a child, after losing several pregnancies and with the physical and emotional toll that took on me, I had reached a point where I thought nothing could shock me anymore. I was wrong.

Reviewing the test results, the acupuncturist's conclusion was simple, and blunt: if I wanted to have a baby, I would have to quit my job. What?! My brain struggled to come to terms with this idea. Essentially, my body was beyond depleted. The stressful combination of my job and multiple miscarriages had wrecked my adrenal glands. My body had produced so much cortisol responding to stressful stimuli that my adrenals had basically worn out. As a result, my body was incapable of sustaining a pregnancy.

Up to that point my career had seemed fine, at least from the outside looking in. I was on a path to increasing levels of responsibility and compensation. However, in quiet moments I realized I wasn't truly happy. When I looked up my ladder, I did not envy or aspire to what I saw.

I spent every day as a cog in a machine, working on a product suite I didn't feel much affinity for, a task that had come to me as I made my way up the ladder. On many days I left work as the sun was going down, realizing that I had not gone outside all day. It all felt kind of ... meh.

Confronted by the stark choice between having a family and keeping this job, something inside me snapped. I had to start being honest with myself. I felt compelled to choose what would leave me feeling the least regret.

With the stakes so high for me, I realized that the only way I could live with the possibility of permanent infertility was to give everything I had to healing my body and providing it the best chance of bearing a child. As I considered the acupuncturist's advice, I suddenly felt myself relax as I realized that I had reached a tipping point. My fear of change had finally been overpowered by my fear of things staying the same.

While it was true that the journey to having a baby was not completely under my control, the direction of my career was. I could elect to change my professional path now, and if a child entered the picture at some point, well, that would be great. But even if I ultimately didn't become a mother, I could create a path to a fulfilling professional life.

That realization, coupled with what the acupuncturist had told me, was the wake-up call I needed to take charge of my career and my life. I could now see that when I was not making deliberate choices about my career, choices were being made for me. I was giving away power. Now I would take that power back.

My wake-up call made me realize that I was in the driver's seat. Over the next six months, before I resigned from my job, my husband and I stopped all discretionary spending and built up our cash reserves. During that time I worked with a career counselor to determine my new professional path. After a sabbatical to heal my body and restore my energy, I entered a two-year certification program for training in my new field, professional coaching. A year later I launched my coaching company. And four years after that I gave birth to my first child.

Since then, I've walked alongside thousands of leaders as they grappled with transforming their professional lives. With my help and support they have asked and answered questions such as, "If I quit, should I take a similar job or make a career change?" Or "How can I make my current job work better for me without blowing up my life?"

Regardless of the form the question takes, professionals have three possible options at this career crossroads:

1. Grow in place, fixing or improving the current job situation.
2. Make a job change, seeking a similar job in a different organization.
3. Start a new career, pursuing a new direction either with the same employer, a different company, or on one's own.

Regardless of which path (or paths) one takes, the underlying theme is the same—wanting something different from what you already have.

No matter how it comes to you, your own wake-up call serves a definite purpose: to get you to pay attention in a new way. Whether you've experienced a health scare, a divorce, a child leaving home, a company reorganization, a job loss, difficult feedback from your boss, or if you've just been procrastinating about a proactive change you've longed for, consider the wake-up call a gift. There's an opportunity to heed that inner guide, the one that's been telling you that you are meant for something more, that you can make a bigger impact, and that you deserve to feel truly engaged in the work you do.

Whether you know the direction you want to go or it remains a mystery, know that you are in control and can make things happen—even if it feels difficult or out of reach right now. This is true even if your plan is to grow where you are.

You may feel a strong desire for professional meaning and a longing to steady yourself in an unsteady world. Here's the good news: right now is a great time to develop a sense of professional agency and turn that sense into reality. There is still time for you to transform your situation, regardless of where you are starting from. You can live a vibrant life through your career, doing your finest work.

Your wake-up call can open doors to a career that is fulfilling, impactful, and successful. And it can be done on your terms. You have within reach the tools you need to reorient yourself and find your footing on the path to where you want to go.

Since you have picked up this book, you probably feel there is room for improvement in your current situation. If you feel called to change your circumstances, this book will walk you through how to muster the courage, create the space, and employ the playbook required to transform your career and your life. The book, and the free tools available at **www.yourfinestwork.com**, will help you create and carry out your action plan to transform your professional life.

Let's now dive into why change is possible, regardless of your age or the stage your career is at. It starts with learning how to become an architect for the next stage of your professional life.

2. BECOME YOUR CAREER'S INTENTIONAL ARCHITECT

From Letting Your Career Happen to You to Taking the Driver's Seat

THE TRAP: ASLEEP AT THE WHEEL

Jennifer was frustrated. As VP of Engineering for a large software company, she watched as another leader got promoted while she was passed over, again. After reporting to four bosses in as many years, she was tired of having to prove herself repeatedly to jockey for an expanded role. After repeating this exercise for what felt like the hundredth time, she decided to look for a new job.

Boy, had it ever been a long time since she conducted a job search!

Having spent over twenty years in her current company, Jennifer found her resume out of date, her headshot in need of an update, and her professional network uncultivated. Although her skills were relevant for her current employer, they were out of synch with what other companies required.

After putting some feelers out, she netted a small number of interviews for jobs that felt so-so to her. It was frustrating to gain such little traction when truly compelling jobs were open. In conversations with recruiters and hiring managers, she struggled to describe her accomplishments. Not surprisingly, her initial efforts did not net her any offers—even for roles she didn't want!

When she was honest with herself, Jennifer realized how exhausted she felt when simply contemplating the idea of an expanded job search. With an overwhelming work schedule and a family at home, how would she find the time and energy to tackle a high-quality search that would result in the career progression she craved? Jennifer was not even 100 percent sure she wanted to leave the company.

Jennifer was caught in the first trap I see with the executives I coach: she was asleep at the wheel. Instead of purposefully driving her career in the direction of her choosing, her experience felt like the tail wagging the dog. She was so busy heads-down doing her job and hoping to be noticed for her good work that she was poorly positioned for proactive change. No wonder she was not getting what she wanted professionally! By not taking control and working things to her advantage, she was letting her career happen to her.

You may be able to relate to Jennifer's story. If you crave a change, you will need to get in the driver's seat. You may be asleep at the wheel too if you:

- feel trapped, passed over, or beholden to your employer

- are gripped by fear you may lose your job
- long for something new but are not sure how to go about achieving it
- are faced with a stale, undeveloped network or personal brand
- have outdated skills

LULLED TO SLEEP OVER TIME

The sense of your career happening to you sets in gradually over time. It is not a conscious decision—in fact, it's the opposite. It is a million little things you don't notice, or course correct for, perhaps over a span of many years. Over time, the impact of these micro decisions, actions, and inactions add up. Since we spend most of our time in reactive mode, inundated by information and things to be done, we often fail to notice how we are floating along on a wave of reactivity and passivity. With the expectations of a 24/7 connected world, we have unprecedented pressures on our work output, response time, and level of reachability. This environment exacerbates the disconnect from our self and what we want for our life.

You may have stumbled into the work you are doing, grounded not in deliberate choices but by circumstances, expectations others have for you, or perhaps even by accident. Over time your attention may have been diverted to establishing and maintaining financial security, growing a family, taking care of aging parents, or other pursuits. You may have grown so accustomed to the benefits and obligations of your life that you haven't been willing to risk "rocking the boat" in your career. All these factors can stack up to make a deliberate career shift a significant challenge.

Some people stay asleep their entire career! Others have the good fortune to experience a wake-up call that snaps them out of their passive state. Once awake, they can see how far they have drifted from the intentional path and choose what to do about it. To take charge takes deliberate energy and effort, pushing against the influx of activity, information, and demands on our attention. Frankly, some are not up for the effort it takes. Others find themselves eager to get started but unsure where to begin. Often, I see situations like Jennifer's; she woke up one day to find that years had gone by without deliberate decisions being made. Suddenly, she felt like she must do something about it—NOW. In cases like hers, the overwhelming feeling of not being able to stand another minute of things staying the way they are is galvanizing.

Though you may sense, in quiet moments, that you are meant for something more, you may not know what to do about it. As a result, when you hear that small whisper, you may ignore it, focusing instead on what is in front of you and what other people—including your employer—want. Over time, your inner voice may grow more insistent and impossible to ignore, building from a gentle hum to a deafening roar.

The internal grumble of career dissatisfaction can grow over time into a physically felt sense, manifesting multi-dimensionally through your thoughts, feelings, and body sensations. It speaks to you earnestly about an area that you have de-emphasized or have resisted addressing. If you ignore it long-term, your body will find other ways to help you pay attention—including, ultimately, a breakdown of your well-being.

Your internal voice may be telling you to:

- reach for something more
- leave a situation
- reduce the effort you are currently putting in
- invest more in a relationship
- take better care of yourself
- quiet your mind
- find a better fit
- use your voice
- nurture your creativity
- believe in yourself
- prioritize what is important to you
- bring more of your true self to your work

Whatever it is telling you, you have a choice about whether to listen and engage.

REDIRECT YOUR ATTENTION TO WHAT'S UNDERNEATH THE SURFACE

When the wake-up call comes and the energy for change is high, it can be tempting to focus on resolving a set of tactical problems versus looking deeper. For Jennifer, she came to me asking for help with her job search and resume. When you hire me, however, you are invited to deepen the inquiry, to look at what is going on beneath the surface. This can feel unfamiliar and even uncomfortable, especially at first. You may find that you resist turning the lens inward and instead focus on reducing the pain you are in as quickly and effortlessly as possible.

Unfortunately, that is not the way sustainable, proactive change happens.

Let's face it—transforming your career is not something you can just think about and "poof," it happens. It requires incremental, consistent activity over a sustained period. To truly evolve your professional life to one in which you hold the reins, you must take a persistent approach, building room and structure for intentional reflection and action into your schedule. This requires you to maintain the tension of "slowing down to speed up."

The effort required is easy to overlook and discount, especially in our instant gratification culture. As a result, you may find yourself in a repeating cycle of:

- feeling the pain of the current situation sharply, a mini wake-up call
- quickly trying a couple things, such as scrolling job listings, reading a couple articles, or sending out a resume or two
- sliding back into complacency and inertia when the immediate discomfort subsides, until the next pain spike occurs

This is not a formula for systemic transformation!

For Jennifer, addressing tactical items such as her resume and interview responses was not the place to start. Instead, she first needed to take responsibility for herself and her journey, clarify what was important to her, and then make that vision come alive, one step at a time.

Plus, she needed to build up her energy and resiliency to be able to weather the effort that such a reflective inquiry—and possible later job search— would require. In her current state, Jennifer was in no shape to be looking for a job; she was not energetically available for a new opportunity. Continuing down this path, she would either remain stuck in her old job or worse—leverage her limited view of herself and her options into a new role that would replicate the current situation—ultimately setting her back farther.

TAKE RESPONSIBILITY FOR YOUR SITUATION

Jennifer berated herself for having been asleep for so long. After twenty years waiting to be recognized for her efforts, she repeatedly watched the credit go to others—including leaders she didn't completely respect.

Now that she had decided to seek a new job elsewhere, she found herself at a disadvantage, having failed to build an active professional network to call upon in her time of need. Not only had Jennifer fallen out of touch with past colleagues and acquaintances, but she had also neglected her professional development. She had kept up with advancements in the company's proprietary technology but not much else. As a result, she had minimal industry contacts and an antiquated skillset.

As she told me how bad things were at work and how poorly her job search was going, yellow caution flags flashed in my head. Jennifer shared her experience as if it were happening without her playing any part in it, like relating the plot of a movie. She saw herself as the subject of the movie but not its director. She was looking to outsource her problem to me to be solved.

My attention softened as I looked past the curt, almost angry way Jennifer was talking to me. When she stopped to take a breath, I asked if I could make an observation. She gasped in relief and said, "Yes, please do," expecting me to share how I would fix her problem for her.

Instead, I voiced my intuitive hit: a sense of sadness emanating off her in waves. Surprised and taken aback, tears began to roll down her cheeks. As her face crumpled and her body relaxed, the details of her grief tumbled out. Jennifer was having trouble getting out of bed in the morning. She was disappointed at not being more successful by this point in her life, felt thwarted by her boss, and frustrated that her leadership did not notice her good work. Jennifer feared she had stayed too long, was too old to start a new chapter, and was trapped in her current, dull situation.

Now we were getting somewhere! We had looked past the surface issues to what lay beneath, peeling back the layers to where her energy was blocked. In my view, Jennifer's biggest issue wasn't her job search; instead, it was the need to take responsibility for her journey to date and take the reins of her career going forward. Only by releasing her attachment to being the victim in her story would she be able to take effective action.

Jennifer needed to heal the disappointment and hurt she felt to be able to move forward. Letting this baggage go would make room for her to get clear on what she wanted next. Both steps were necessary for her eventual job search to be successful.

PRACTICES AND TACTICS

The key reframe for becoming your career's intentional architect is to decide to take charge of your situation. Regardless of your circumstances and what has come before, you can make the decision right now to take the reins of your career and turn it in the direction of your choosing. Whether growing in place, making a job change, or launching a career pivot, your aim is to increase your sense of *control*, taking responsibility for your professional life and being in charge of where you head from here. You can pair the following practices and tactics with the free bonus tools available at **www.yourfinestwork.com** to improve your sense of control.

Invite yourself to the party

The path to career fulfillment is there for the taking, but you must proactively step into it. Whether you are a pragmatic person or a bit more on the reserved side, it can be especially tempting to sit back and wait, thinking that you will:

- do good work, and advancement opportunities will naturally appear
- speak up in the leadership meeting when someone calls on you
- meet with a peer to network when he or she invites you for coffee
- discuss your career with your boss when the subject comes up naturally
- start working in a new job when someone recruits you
- make a career pivot when an opportunity arises

It is tempting to wait to live a meaningful life through your career until it is handed to you or magically appears. That is *not* the way things work. Instead, the path to career fulfillment is paved with opportunities you create on your own.

So, instead of the list above, in reality, it reads more like this:

Instead of: Expecting your work to speak for itself, and advancement opportunities to naturally appear

Do this: Do good work while also connecting the dots for your boss to understand that you would like to advance; initiate proactive discussions to identify gaps between where you are and where you need to be to be considered for advancement, and then actively work to close them.

Instead of: Speaking up in the leadership meeting when someone calls on you

Do this: Speak up in the leadership meeting each session, ideally within the first five minutes, to get your voice in the room. Even if all you do is ask a though-provoking, open ended question to move the conversation forward, be clear on what you stand for, and speak up proactively to move your agenda forward as well as to support your colleagues.

Instead of: Meeting with your peers to network whenever one invites you for coffee

Do this: Invite your peers for regular networking touchpoints, co-creating an agenda that makes it valuable for both of you to prioritize meeting.

Instead of: Starting to work in a new job when someone recruits you

Do this: Reach out to your network to bring them up to speed with where you are headed next. Update your professional positioning to make a compelling case for you being a good fit for the role you seek. Find ways to get exposure to and into conversation with those in a position of influence to help you access the roles you are targeting so they remember you when they are sourcing candidates for roles.

Instead of: Making a career pivot when an opportunity arises

Do this: Proactively try on and move into a new arena, volunteering, taking courses, joining professional associations, and/or working on a self-initiated project that makes a compelling case for the future you want.

The momentum you build over time by taking baby steps on your own behalf ushers in what you are longing for. Sitting back and waiting to be invited is a path to futility.

Make time to stare out the window

David was feeling underwhelmed in his job as a senior technology leader. A natural visionary, he had more ideas than he knew what to do with and not enough time to noodle them. His job kept him running from one meeting to the next all day long, helping the machine go. Over time, he found his level of satisfaction at work falling, something he shared in one of our coaching conversations.

"How would you like to be spending your time?" I asked him. "What is the dream?"

Reflecting, David responded, "If I could spend half my time supporting projects in the portfolio, a third mentoring my direct reports, and the balance of my time 'staring out the window,' that would feel great."

David's passion was pioneering new ground, whether fleshing out new concepts or finding ways to deliberately disrupt what his company was doing to provide competitive advantage. Sitting in his office staring off into space provided the opportunity to think through his more abstract ideas. During this time, he could bring form to the concepts and opportunities that flitted in and out of his brain and then act on them. Two of his seemingly amorphous ideas had been transformed into tangible, results-driving outcomes benefiting the company. Even with this concrete evidence of success in hand, however, he found himself spending minimal scheduled time "thinking the big thoughts."

With this new awareness, David carved out a chunk of time two mornings a week to sit undisturbed in his office, pondering how to solve the complex problems his customers and teams were facing. With this small shift, his work satisfaction shot up considerably. It required him to tighten his schedule, to find ways to be more efficient with delegation, prioritize which meetings to attend, and to get more done in less time, but he felt motivated to make these trade-offs.

When leaders institute staring-out-the-window time as a practice, they often ask me, "But what do I spend the time *doing?*" I answer, "You don't *do*. You spend your time *being*." You close down all the ways that people can get to you—and you to them—and sit quietly, centering yourself. From that quiet place, you determine the areas that most need your focus to make a considerable difference. Staring-out-the-window time brings you into alignment with your true talents, interests, professional charter, and opportunities. It keeps you awake to the intentional path versus the one that you may have automatically followed over the years.

Intrigued? Here's how to do it:

1. Pick a one- to two-hour time slot, book it in your calendar, and let others know it is off-limits. Make it a recurring weekly meeting. If you are not able to devote time during your workday, architect it into your weekly schedule another way.

2. Go analog. Get off your computer and phone for this sacred time. Pull out a whiteboard, blank pieces of paper, or a set of sticky notes to play with on a blank wall. Whatever is different from your regular mode of working. You may also want to sit in a different spot.

3. Mentally review your key priorities, culling the huge pile on your professional plate. Confirm what are the most energizing and important for you to

pay attention to, whether it's leadership development, your role's charter, or your career fulfillment.
Float between those areas of importance or pick
a lane and focus on just one.

A sample big thinking session might include elements
like these:

- Reflect on what you want and need to continue to
  be engaged and choose to remain in this company,
  this job, and this line of work.
- Read a book, white paper, or article on a topic you
  are interested in and then synthesizing the learnings to apply on the job.
- Script a conversation to have with your boss to
  advocate for yourself and what you really want or
  an initiative you believe in.
- Consider what to start, stop, and continue doing to
  achieve the highest leverage point in your job and
  making an action plan to translate those ideas into
  real-life practice.

Creating time to stare out the window is an essential
component of doing your finest work. By regularly inter-
rupting the pattern of reactivity that comes with the
ongoing demands on your time and attention, you can
zoom in on what is most important regarding your key
priorities for your career, leadership development, and the
constituents you serve.

THE VIEW FROM THE DRIVER'S SEAT

With coaching, Jennifer stepped back to confirm what she most wanted in her next role so she could recognize it when she found it. She was accustomed to being reactive to what others wanted rather than thinking proactively on her own behalf. Reflecting on what mattered most to her reaffirmed her commitment to crafting a role that incorporated the elements she held dear.

At the same time, Jennifer began taking better care of herself. She met with her medical doctor to diagnose what she had long suspected—that she was suffering from mild depression. As Jennifer started on medication to treat it, she also made room in her schedule to rejuvenate her energy. She rearranged her workspace at home to be able to close off work at the end of the day and restarted an enjoyable hobby she had let go by the wayside. With the uplift from these activities, Jennifer next turned her attention to making work take less effort in order to preserve her time and energy.

Only once she had boosted her sense of well-being and clarified her career target did Jennifer update her professional story to incorporate the years of undocumented accomplishments. She educated herself about the modern job search, enrolled in training courses to upgrade her skills to match industry standards, and connected with people in positions of influence. She also had a professional photographer take a new headshot to showcase her as the executive she truly was.

Rather than continue to be lulled by her current situation, Jennifer positioned herself for her next move internally, advocating for additional responsibility and offering to lead initiatives in emerging areas. She spent significant time studying new technologies; this new knowledge gave her a big confidence boost and the ability to propose novel product development approaches. She found it critically important to spend time studying, especially outside her realm of expertise, to keep sight of where the market was headed. Her takeaway: if you spend too much time doing an excellent job in your current area, you can get left behind. She vowed to never let that happen again.

Her employer took notice of her professional and technical upgrade, as well as her newfound confidence. As she entertained options for new roles with other companies, she was offered a promotion and larger scope of responsibility by her current employer. Ultimately, she decided to stay there, this time on her terms.

The satisfaction of evolving from feeling trapped and without a sense of control to negotiating intentionally for what you truly want and deserve is priceless. Waking up, connecting with yourself, identifying what you want, and then putting those criteria out in the universe so they can materialize for you is a transformative experience.

3. DEFINE YOUR OWN NORTH STAR

*From Scattered and Reactive to
Crystal Clear About What You Want*

THE TRAP: FOCUSED ON EVERYONE'S AGENDA BUT YOUR OWN

As Chris answered emails at 2 AM, a familiar sense of shame washed over him. Why did he repeatedly give up his personal time—and sleep—to take care of other people's priorities? This question was followed closely by another—what options did he have? He felt backed into a corner without a viable alternative.

As VP of Customer Experience, married, and the father of three young children, Chris found himself constantly spread too thin at work. All day long he moved from meeting to meeting, removing obstacles blocking his large, multi-faceted team's ability to fulfill their ambitious charter. In his prior role at the company, he had owned one piece of the Customer Experience (CX) organization. With a recent promotion he had tripled his span of responsibility, employees, and functions, with more objectives and key results (OKRs).

The company clearly believed in him and his ability to get things done. So why didn't he feel better about his ability to fulfill his potential? Every direction he looked, there were things to be done. As a result, Chris felt on edge, scattered, and reactive. On the rare occasion when he found himself with a short window of time to get something done, he could barely focus!

On a day-to-day basis, Chris felt like an imposter, aware that although he was busy, he was not pushing the company's strategic objectives he was responsible for. Instead, he focused on what was in front of him: urgent demands from his team, peers, leaders, and customers. He stayed on top of things, walking alongside his direct reports to block and tackle so they felt supported. As a result, he enjoyed a reputation as a caretaker of others, a distinction he enjoyed and felt committed to maintaining.

Given how hard he was working, it felt disheartening to receive 360-degree feedback from his superiors, peers, and subordinates that he was not viewed as a true executive leader. The collective insight was that he was neither using his voice to drive change at the highest level nor sufficiently driving the CX charter. How could he, he wondered, given his heavy workload? There was never enough time to work systematically on the important stuff. At the same time he understood, in his heart of hearts, that their feedback was justified. He wanted to do something about it without compromising service to his team and customers. This left him feeling stuck and unsure how to proceed.

Chris was suffering from the second trap I see leaders fall into—being on everyone's agenda but one's own. Although he prioritized maintaining strong relationships and staying on top of day-to-day operational details, his ethos seemed to be, "You need me to jump? How high?" He spent his time shapeshifting to address whoever was shouting loudest. As a result, he was not able to fulfill his professional potential, at least from the perspective of his colleagues.

Do you feel like you are constantly overextending yourself and doing others' work? Are you losing precious time in a barrage of meetings, reacting to what is being asked of you, and vaguely aware that you are not working to your true abilities? If so, like Chris, you may also be focused from the outside in. To regain a sense of control, you will need to get crystal clear about what you want from your job and career, define your personal North Star, and then let it guide you from the inside out.

CONNECT WITH WHAT YOU REALLY WANT

Contemplating what you desire for your career can evoke fear, excitement, and uncertainty, especially if it is the first time you have given yourself permission to consider your preferences. I ask the professionals I coach what they would change if they could wave a magic wand and have things exactly as they please, career-wise. Often, the question catches them by surprise. It may take you aback too; in fact, you may not even be able to muster an answer. At best, the dream may look blurry. For some it is so uncomfortable to consider this line of inquiry that they are tempted to redirect their focus to tactical actions rather than truly transformational strategies.

Each coaching engagement I embark on is as unique as the individual person being coached. However, coaching *always* begins with us clarifying what the individual wants from their career. Just as if we were building a house, the structure must rest on a firm foundation. In virtually all cases, I find that this foundation is not built on solid ground when we start; rather, the picture is typically fuzzy and short on details. My job is to help my executive clients transform the picture from a pencil sketch into a full painting. I want their career vision to have a visceral, alluring quality to it. That way, the vision will pull them forward and help them take focused action to bring it into being.

Most often, a person comes to coaching claiming not to know what they want. That is their conscious mind talking. In actuality, they have the answers inside of them; we just need to find a way to bring these answers to their awareness and arrange them in a form that feels practical and actionable.

In Chris's case he felt a bit disconnected from his desires for his career, focused instead on taking care of his team and not disappointing his superiors. Those qualities, though clearly important to him, emphasize what *others* want from Chris, not what *he* wants from and for himself. This is a critical shift to make when defining your North Star. Just like a captain in a stormy sea focuses attention on the horizon to right the boat and chart a path through the storm, your North Star trains your eye on your own personal horizon. That way you can course correct as you navigate your day-to-day work experiences.

Although Chris intended to stay and grow in his current company, he was disillusioned by the feedback he'd received. He wanted to strengthen his strategic abilities but did not know where to start. When we discussed clarifying his personal career priorities, he didn't at first grasp how it would translate into helping him become more strategic and leader-like on the job, but he was game to try.

To start, Chris inventoried what was important to him in his career, including his top values and how he would know when each one was honored in his work environment. He had a challenging time reducing his values down to five but with some tradeoffs finally got there. A lightbulb went off when he realized that three of the five qualities he most prized were not in line with his current situation.

We focused on what he could do to shift the values into alignment, finding some easier to address than others. Together we devised experiments to run, practices to adopt, and requests he could make of others to begin to move the out-of-alignment values to the "honored" column.

LEARN FROM WHAT YOU *DON'T* WANT

It's easy to get discouraged, especially when your current or most recent job feels suboptimal. However, our best clues to what we want going forward are often rooted in the distasteful and disappointing experiences we have walked through in the past.

As Chris and I turned our attention to the attributes of his ideal work environment, he referenced traits that represented what he *didn't* want, rather than what he *did*. For example, he didn't want to share leadership responsibilities with another person. This mirrored his current situation, where he co-led the CX function with another leader. The other person was more extroverted than Chris and proactively served as mouthpiece to the C-suite for their combined team. That irked him.

"Okay, if that is what you *don't* want, turn it on its head," I told him.

"What do you mean by that?" Chris responded.

"We are creating a vision of what you want to move *toward*, not what you want to move *away* from. So, if this is something you *don't* like in your work environment, state the opposite, because that inherently will describe something that you *do* like."

Chris thought about it and clarified that he wanted sole authority and leadership of his area. He needed a straight line to the C-suite, with regular communication, facetime, and feedback loops. As he fleshed out his vision, Chris continued to turn things on their head when he encountered elements that he found draining. Beyond his top values and ideal work environment, he named preferred job duties, favorite skills to use, areas of satisfaction, desired compensation, and other data points to create a robust picture of his ideal career.

As Chris's image of his optimal work came into sharp focus, some attributes felt beyond his control, while others felt personally actionable. However, identifying what he truly wanted began to reveal how he could influence even those elements that seemed beyond his control.

REORIENT YOUR ATTENTION

When I first start coaching an executive, they state their problem and what makes them feel stuck. Regardless of framing, it boils down to the seeming inability to gain access to what they want. They naturally focus on apparent blockers to reaching their goals. Most often, these elements appear to be beyond their control.

In my experience, this type of focus leads to nothing good. Although some things may indeed be *outside* of your control, you can still *influence* them. And a lot of things are actually *within* your control, especially when you orient your attention first to what you want. In fact, doing so is the best place to start. Conducting an inventory of your vision for your career helps you bring it into being. With this clarity on your personal priorities, you can re-engage with what others want from you. This dual focus automatically balances the energetic scale between what you want and what others need, so that you feel more grounded and focused.

If you start with what others want for you, you end up in a situation that contains qualities *you* don't want but that *others* want or need, like Chris did. Conversely, if you exclusively focus on what *you* want, you end up being pie-in-the-sky and unrealistic. The overlap between these two sets of data points is where the magic is, offering work that both delights you and meets the wants and needs of others. Do it in this order: 1) identify what you want and then 2) confirm what others need from you. This ensures that you don't shoot too low in your aspirations but rather ground yourself in your heart's desire first and foremost. The powerful place to position yourself is at the intersection of these two dynamics.

You can still be practical and target how to achieve the promotion, improve your situation, or be an attractive candidate for your ideal job. You just first need to get clear on what you want. When you illuminate your personal priorities, you stand up straighter and naturally exude more gravitas. This in turn makes you a more appealing prospect to those in a position to help you access and do your finest work.

If this orientation on what you want is the best, most strategic place to start, why don't more people start there? For one, we have not been trained to think this way—rather, we have spent our careers problem-solving within constraints on behalf of our companies. As a result, we are not used to blue-sky thinking. Further, many leaders I coach—including Chris—were raised to be humble. For these folks, prioritizing what you want and then taking action to get it, including showcasing your skills and accomplishments, can feel like bragging. However, helping people understand the value you create is critical to opening doors to more of what you want. The trick is to do so in line with your values; for those who find this challenging, the easiest way to shift this reluctance is to discuss how your professional contributions create benefit for others.

PRACTICES AND TACTICS

There are a lot of things that you can do with your career—it's what you *want* to do that matters. You may tend to overlook or not allow yourself the time, space, and structure to explore what you truly yearn for, instead focusing on what you are good at or what others need from you. It's important to pay attention to the latter but only *after* running it through the filter of what you truly desire for yourself. The goal is to increase your sense of *clarity*, establishing a deep foundation in what you know to be true and important to you personally. This reduces the scattered feeling and helps you stop second-guessing yourself. You can pair these practices and tactics with the free bonus tools at **www.yourfinestwork.com** to clarify where you are starting from and where you most need to focus your attention.

Think without limits ... initially

When embarking on any career-related endeavor, I invite you to pause, take a breath, and make room for blue-sky thinking. Rather than limit yourself right out of the gate, consider embarking on an open-minded exploration of what you most desire from the change. There will be time to be practical later!

Here are a few questions to get you started. Consider journaling your answers to them and see where the inquiry takes you.

- What do I want from this next chapter career-wise?
- What energizes me?
- What drains me?
- What do I welcome more of?
- What do I want less of?
- How do I want to be of service to others?
- What type of outcomes do I want to make possible with my work?
- Who do I want to become?

This process shifts your attention from the expectations others have of you to what you consider essential aspects of career satisfaction. Once you have identified these qualities, you can spot them when exploring career opportunities.

Compile and road test your top values

The path to career fulfillment is through your values. When you are dissatisfied with your situation, the first place to look is your top values and how they are either aligned or not aligned with the way you are living and working now.

Although many of your values remain stable throughout your life, others change as your circumstances evolve. For example, in his twenties and thirties, Roger valued mobility, loving to travel for work; when he married in his early forties, he found that the need for stability outranked his desire to be on the go. It is good practice to review your top values at least once a year to see how they are evolving and how you are applying them.

When contemplating a change, we automatically look for something at least as good as what we have now (or had in our last role). It follows, then, that one way to increase your satisfaction at work is to bring your top out-of-sync values into alignment. For example, let's say you prioritize having balance but find yourself working all hours of the day and without time to decompress and enjoy your life outside of work. Devoting attention and effort into shifting those dynamics is a high-return activity.

Consider compiling your own top values, selecting the ones that feel especially motivating to you regardless of whether they are currently being lived out in the way you work. Start with a larger list and then narrow it down to your top five, prioritized in order of importance. A further step is to review the top five against your current work situation—or most recent job if you are currently in between roles—to see how they measure up regarding your lived experience of the job. Is your current situation meeting your expectations values-wise, or is your reality the opposite of what you prioritize? Make a note of what you observe.

One of three patterns will emerge. Either you will find that:

- most of your top values are honored
- most are nonexistent
- it's almost an even split

If most of your top values are present, you may find yourself feeling a bit ambivalent about making a change, though on hard days you may long for something different. This tension makes sense given that you are largely working in alignment with your leading values. So it may not be the ideal time to make a full-scale change unless you can harness meaning and motivation from somewhere else. Rather, consider laying the groundwork for a future shift while making smaller tweaks to your current situation to improve your satisfaction in the near term.

If most of your top values are *not* present, you are obviously in pain and may feel driven to make a change in the short- to medium-term. You are well-served by considering a triple focus: 1) endeavoring to bring your most prized values into alignment as much as possible within your current role, assuming you have energy for it;

2) launching extra-curricular projects or hobbies to honor your top values in other areas of your life; and 3) laying the groundwork for a change to your role, organization, or field.

If you have an almost even split, you may feel torn, asking yourself, "Should I *stay* or should I *go*?" Your path to peace may include a side activity that fulfills your values. In addition, you may choose to split your time between incubating a future change and making incremental improvements where you are.

Perhaps the most powerful step in the values inquiry is the final one—identifying evidence that tells you when each of your top values is in alignment with your work environment. Your goal here is aspirational, identifying how you would *like* things to be, so you can learn to recognize—and create—a promising container in which to do your finest work.

For many mid-career executives, career satisfaction is significantly influenced by the way colleagues treat each other, how employees are recognized, and the company's mission and culture. Don't be surprised if this is the case for you—so pay special attention to these elements. For example, Sarah sought a new employer that prioritized "learning," as evidenced by "clear investment in the professional development of employees."

Unsure if the company she was interviewing with would honor this value, Sarah asked, "What do I do if my target employer's approach doesn't meet my requirements? Do I decline the opportunity?"

My answer: *not necessarily*.

Sarah may decide to still take the job, provided the role offers enough of a match with her other criteria. She can gauge the company's appetite to invest in a learning-based culture, including supporting employee development. Sarah can offer—and negotiate before coming onboard—to help instill this culture. Alternatively, she can build in learning *outside* her job, either through volunteer work, a Board seat, book or blog writing, a side hustle, or a line of study in an area of professional interest.

Bottom line: if an employment opportunity does not support a cherished value and you decide to take the position anyway, the need for alignment does not go away. You just need to get creative about how you build it into your work and life.

Your top values, once identified, become a beacon. In fact, you may find yourself more uncomfortable once you identify where the elements of your current situation are at odds with what is most important to you. Sometimes, value mismatches can be repaired; other times they cannot. Having your short list front and center helps you make the determination between the two. Best practice is to make your top values visible every day. One executive I know displays them in his email signature; another leader stenciled hers around her bathtub.

Here are some sample values, with examples of how a leader knows when they are being respected:

- **Leadership** = I have autonomy in how I run my team. I set the direction and create the culture. I'm known in my industry for my thought leadership. I have an impact on other teams, leaders, the broader company culture, and business decisions.

- **Dependability** = Colleagues, friends, and family feel close because we are communicating and collaborating. I feel trust in these relationships because I know I am delivering what is expected of me, and I know I can rely on those around me at all levels.
- **Balance** = I have energy at both work and home to take on challenges and opportunities. I do not feel frazzled, tired, or burned out.
- **Meaningful Work** = What I do contributes to a better future for humanity. My work is connected to core topics I am passionate about, such as social equity and environmental protection. My employer helps people on a global scale. I can speak about what I do with others—and with my kids—and feel proud.
- **Developing Potential** = I have influence about what I'm developing. I am demonstrating my potential in ways that are a direct outgrowth of my work, conversations with leaders, and support I receive. I feel positive and excited to take on more because I *want* to, not because I *must*. My team members are excelling and demonstrating their potential in ways that are a direct result of my support and that of other leaders.

If you do decide to move on from your role, your top values become key areas to probe in job and informational interviews. This allows you to sleuth out the degree to which the new employment situation will be a good fit and enable your finest work.

Identify your non-negotiables and measures of success

Debbie came to coaching dreading going to work each day. Her chief complaint: her commute took her an hour outside San Francisco, where she both lived and longed to work. This, among other elements, led her to decide to leave her current role and secure a new job. However, Debbie had trouble articulating what she wanted beyond the requirement that the job be in the city. Her thoughts were scattered, making it difficult to imagine a better fit. I invited her to stop looking outward at job postings and start looking inward instead.

With structure and support, Debbie reflected on what was personally important for her next role, walking through past experiences to identify themes about what she enjoyed doing and where she thrived. A picture gradually emerged of requirements for potential job opportunities. Debbie refined her criteria further to a prioritized set of non-negotiables, representing what she absolutely needed to have to say *yes* to a new opportunity.

Debbie's non-negotiables guided her targeted job search, networking, and interviewing efforts. Since she was purposeful and focused, her search progressed quicker than prior efforts, culminating in three offers she compared before accepting the best fit for her finest work.

Here's how to identify *your* non-negotiables. Start by outlining the following elements and then further refine the most important aspects across your answers into a prioritized list.

Reflect and journal on:

- values of top importance
- skills you most want to use
- aspects of your personality you need to feel comfortable showing at work to feel like you are being yourself
- the type of work environment that supports your finest work
- how you would like to derive satisfaction from work
- job duties you want to perform
- competencies you enjoy and want to employ on the job
- the types of business problems you feel energized to solve
- interests you have that you would like the work to support
- the compensation package you need and want

You can use your non-negotiables as a rubric for making intentional, strategic career decisions. You can compare your current role with them to reveal where priorities are at risk and train your attention on opportunities to close the gap between what you have and what you want. When considering a new role, you can measure your options against your non-negotiables to identify a likely fit and areas to further probe. Gaps between your non-negotiables and a potential job offer can be explored with open-ended, thoughtful questions designed to clarify whether an element you prize is likely to be present.

To use your non-negotiables effectively, determine your

measures of success. In other words, how will you know that a particular requirement is met? For example, one of Debbie's must-haves was "a seat at the leadership table." She defined this requirement as being met when the role:

- was graded at the senior leadership level
- required participation in the weekly leadership meeting
- offered regular one-on-one facetime with her boss and skip level manager
- supported at least one of the top three challenges of the company
- fell in a company whose culture invites employees to contribute ideas and those ideas were taken seriously by the C-suite

When interviewing for a new role or advocating for advancement, Debbie verified the degree to which what was on offer met her requirements.

FROM VISION TO REALITY

Chris' reflection clarified that although he valued responsiveness to others' needs, he was also truly invested in being seen as a driver of strategic priorities for the company. Realizing he had overinvested in one area and underinvested in others, Chris found ways to assert his authority and perspective with the C-suite. He made it a practice to speak up in leadership meetings and instituted two-way feedback loops via regular one-on-one meetings with peers and superiors.

With his North Star guiding him, Chris found ways to clearly convey the need to cease the co-leadership arrangement. He successfully made the argument to benefit not only his personal preferences but also to produce better outcomes for the company.

As he blended his personal priorities with the feedback he had received, Chris initially became overwhelmed with so much on his plate. To make room for the additional effort his new focus required, he needed to turn his attention away from some of what others needed from him.

The breakthrough came when he defined ways to care for his team by putting the onus on them to manage their *own* needs. Chris shortened some meetings, dropped or consolidated others, and trained his direct reports to prioritize their requests of him in one-on-one meetings. He helped the larger team refine processes for tackling typical scenarios, eliminating duplicate work for himself and others. Chris reframed his mandate to help his team become increasingly self-sufficient, engaged, and empowered, while he focused on strategic pursuits.

In many cases, you can make your current situation more fulfilling, impactful, and successful, at least to a degree. Instead of turning your focus to what *others* need from you, first turn your attention toward a better understanding of what *you* want from this stage of your career and beyond. Then and only then will you know what levers to push to make improvements for you and others. Doing so can also help you decide whether to grow where you are or make a change to a new opportunity.

4. FILL YOUR TANK

From Burned Out and Exhausted to
a Lightened Load and Restored Energy

THE TRAP: RUNNING ON EMPTY

As the alarm chirped, Jeff reflexively hit the snooze button. Thirty minutes later the fog of sleep lifted, and a sense of heaviness descended on his chest. He dragged himself out of bed, muttering to his husband, "Monday mornings are the worst." Briefly wondering if calling in sick was possible, Jeff skipped exercising yet again and instead grabbed a cup of coffee and took a hot shower. Even with those pick-me-ups, he felt exhausted logging in to begin the workday.

Jeff's attention was consumed by several key deliverables, including drafting the marketing strategy for the new product launch. It was a complex project that required detailed thought to do well—something he had neither the energy nor the motivation to tackle. Jeff considered delegating some of the work to the team but resisted doing so, knowing the group was already overextended.

As Jeff plodded through the day, he felt a tightness in his chest and a headache coming on. Why did the light seem so bright? He regretted staying up too late bingeing on his latest Netflix obsession.

Looking at the day's schedule, Jeff discovered that the annual budget was past due, and he hadn't even started putting it together! With a full inbox and several fires to put out, he felt unsure where to find the energy or time to craft the budget. Ugh. He resolved to start the budgeting process tomorrow. He grabbed a piece of chocolate to help him wake up.

A dim thought surfaced: the need for a change. Perhaps a new job, a career transition, a sabbatical, or even a vacation. How to choose? Where to start? Jeff felt the fog descend again. He would have to think about those things later. Now, he was late for the next meeting to discuss the pressing issue of the day. As Jeff logged into the Zoom call, he fumbled his apologies for being late yet again.

Jeff suffered from the third trap I see executives fall into—running on empty. He dragged himself through his days, dazed and feeling a sense of dread.

If you feel like you are wiped out and crave a change but can barely manage to get through *your* day, you are probably suffering from burnout and exhaustion. To fix this you will need to first focus on lightening your load and restoring your energy, "filling your tank." By this I mean that you replenish and maintain your level of emotional, physical, intellectual, and spiritual energy.

REALIZE YOU HAVE SPOONS TO SPEND

Spoon theory, conceived by a woman suffering from Lupus, is the idea that we each have a limited supply of energy in any given day. You start each day with a certain number of spoons, each one indicating a level of intention, effort, energy, and focus available for you to use. Throughout the day, as you do different things, you "spend" your spoons. When all of them are gone, you are mentally, emotionally, and physically done for the day. If your health is compromised and/or if you are under stress, you may start the day with fewer spoons. The idea is to use them wisely.

When you find yourself in a place like Jeff did, the symptoms may manifest as feeling drained, unmotivated, or buffeted about. Regardless of form, the impact is the same: exhaustion, stress, depletion, a lack of creativity, and apparently limited options to fix the situation. Basically, you are out of spoons. Left unchecked, these conditions can lead to serious health problems. They are signals that you need to heed the warnings they represent.

When you find yourself in this place or close to it, you may be tempted to try to discipline yourself out of it. For example, trying to exercise more or bearing down and working harder to get more done in less time. However, this approach typically doesn't work because it requires energy you don't have. You can't solve the problem of running on empty by *doing* yourself out of it. Rather, the path forward is through your state of *being*.

BE WILLING TO SURRENDER

My all-time favorite guided meditation is by storyteller and meditation teacher Sarah Blondin. I've listened to her eight-minute "Learning to Surrender" meditation so many times I almost have it memorized. The message I take from her wise words is that there are times when we just need to let go, times when we need to slow down rather than to speed up, to stop trying to hold everything and to just let things fall where they are and rest. There are times when we need to realize that regardless of our spiritual beliefs, there are forces beyond our will at work. We are surrounded by energy that holds us and draws us ever toward more of what we want—when we just let it happen. To access this energy, we simply need to loosen our grip, let go, and let the flow of life's river take us along—to stop fighting, to stop straining, and simply surrender.

This message is so powerful. Yet, you may find you resist it, as it feels counterintuitive, especially as you endeavor to get ahead in your career. However, when you are in what feels like survival mode, this call to surrender can be a balm for the soul. It can feel like a window opening when a door closes.

We spend so much of our time at work focused on our thinking. Surrendering comes from truly inhabiting our bodies. How do you do this? Again, it's not a state of *doing*— it's a state of *being*. It's changing the quality and focus of your attention. Surrendering involves shifting your focus down your body, from your head to your heart and eventually to your gut. It involves checking with your intuition before taking any action, counting on your inner guide to inform your choices. By the way, this is not a one-time thing—it is a practice that you may need to repeat 100 or 1000 times a day. By redirecting your attention from your *thinking* mind to your *feeling* body, you ground—and re-ground—yourself.

In real life, surrendering looks like recognizing your energetic limits and honoring them. It may mean not logging back in to your email to do more work at night after the kids go to bed or you've finished dinner. It may look like going to sleep earlier and getting up earlier to focus on tasks that take you less time to complete in the morning than in the evening. It may look like eliminating meetings from your schedule, sending a delegate for sessions that can't be canceled, or reducing the length or frequency of other checkpoints. It may look like extending the project deadline or reducing its scope. It may look like resigning from a board or volunteer role that you have held because you felt obligated but that drains you. Surrendering is ultimately about *belief.* Belief that if you don't check your email or respond to that ping from your boss right away, the sky will not fall. If you prioritize taking care of yourself, you will neither lose out nor let other people down. If you slow down, take a breath, and take care of yourself, you will be safe. If you find more efficient ways to do things and make them take less from you, it doesn't mean you are slacking. If you empower others to do tasks that historically only you have done and/or you can do better or faster than others, you will not negate your value. If you take a moment to breathe, focus on being in your body and stop being consumed by the crisis of the moment, you will ultimately be more effective.

MAKE EVERYTHING TAKE LESS

It takes spoons to transform your situation. When you are overwhelmed and under-resourced, your spoons are typically in short supply. To end your feeling of depletion, you need to reclaim some of those spoons. You do that by taking things off your plate and reducing the effort your current workload and lifestyle require of you. That can feel almost impossible at the outset, but there are lots of small ways to do it.

I often find that executives I coach feel like they are juggling multiple balls and that none of them can drop. To them, these balls seem like they are made of glass; if any fall, they will break. What an exhausting way to work and live! It is neither a sustainable workstyle nor a helpful mindset. When you are running on empty, you likely need to proactively put some of the balls down or let them go. Instead of glass, imagine the balls are made of rubber. What happens when you drop one—or more? They don't shatter, they bounce.

A primary strategy to reclaim spoons as a leader is to put the work where it belongs—on your team—and not take on so much yourself. This approach benefits your employees, helping them become more engaged in driving outcomes. Burned-out Jeff benefited from this strategy, claiming back time in his schedule while empowering others. Once Chris, the overwhelmed CX leader, became clear on his North Star, he changed the way he interacted with his direct reports to have them take more responsibility for themselves.

What does it look like to put the work where it belongs as an executive? It looks like having your direct reports hold the agenda for their one-on-ones with you. It's up to *them* to get what they need from you! It looks like setting clear expectations for each project with escalation procedures for the team to activate if agreed-upon delivery is in jeopardy. It looks like taking stock of the types of decisions you *need* to weigh in on, and letting go of those you *don't*, establishing ongoing feedback loops to stay connected while floating above the details. Assuming you have an assistant, it looks like tasking them with arranging your schedule to reclaim three hours per week, and then reserve that time for your professional development and larger issues that make a material difference for the organization. It looks like directing your team members to evaluate their slate of projects and make recommendations on where to cut scope, extend deadlines, or shutter initiatives altogether.

One of the hardest things to do, especially when running on empty, is to let your team step up and do the work. It can be tempting to think you are the only one who has the answers and who can do the best job with important tasks. However, working sustainably requires leveraging your talents to make others successful rather than trying to drive everything yourself. It requires understanding and embracing that you produce better outcomes for the company when you harness the power of others and don't spread yourself too thinly.

Even if you are still emerging as a leader, the spirit is the same: surrendering to the fact that you can't do it all. This may mean renegotiating projects and deadlines, streamlining tasks and responsibilities, or setting and honoring boundaries to protect your precious energy. Although it's easier said than done, with sufficient motivation these shifts are possible.

When you have direct reports with different personalities and communication styles than you do, it can be especially tempting to jump in and do the work yourself rather than navigate the differences in style. However, even when you are running on empty, there are ways to effectively put the work where it belongs.

A busy senior digital leader, Maria felt irritated that her direct report, Ruth, filled their interactions with complaints and unnecessary detail. Each week she found herself dreading their one-on-one meeting and other conversations, unsure how to make their interactions shorter and more to the point. Why couldn't Ruth just bottom-line things like her peers did?

Maria came to our coaching session exasperated after a written exchange with Ruth. While both women completed heavy, urgent prep for an upcoming event launch for the company, Ruth reached out to ask for some of Maria's time. Maria responded by saying, "I'm really busy with these company event details; can it wait until our one-on-one next week?"

When Ruth responded, "Yes," Maria breathed a sigh of relief, thinking the exchange was over. However, Ruth proceeded to send a long message detailing things going on for her and her team, in effect ignoring the "let's wait until next week" decision.

This is where Maria made a critical miscalculation. She took the bait and responded to the message, answering what she guessed was the question buried in Ruth's long list of updates. Maria wasn't sure, but she just needed it dealt with so she could return to her true priorities. Maria's annoyance spiked when Ruth responded, telling her why her recommendations to solve the problem would not work and adding even greater detail. It ended up being an unsatisfying interaction for both women and an unneeded distraction from urgent launch prep.

As Maria and I deconstructed the interchange, it became clear that she had missed an opportunity. The situation reminded me of a young child asking their parents for something repeatedly and the parents saying "no," emphatically at first but later giving in. The lesson the child learns: to persist with the asking, wearing their parents down until they eventually get what they want.

The opportunity missed was to have Ruth manage herself and her needs, in the moment. The path to success for Ruth as a leader is to guide her to take responsibility for herself. Maria can do this by asking Ruth to state her need clearly and refuse to engage in other nonessential elements of conversation in the moment. Until Maria adopted this change, the behavior that frustrated her in her direct report would persist.

PRACTICES AND TACTICS

The path to your finest work is not accessible by sacrificing your health and well-being for the job. Once you can see and accept that concept, then you can take steps to correct the imbalances in your situation and regain your energy. Your goal is to increase your *stamina* so you can proceed on the journey to your finest work. Stamina provides you with the room and energy to implement the strategies, practices, and tactics in this book, lightening your load so you can proactively move in the direction of your choice. Consider using the following practices and tactics along with the free tools at **www.yourfinestwork.com** to focus your precious energy and attention.

Determine where to spend your spoons

Imagine you are preparing for an extended road trip by car. As part of your departure planning, you make sure to have everything you need. You confirm the car's tires are adequately inflated, the gas tank is full, and necessary supplies, including devices, power cords, clothes, snacks, and toiletries, are packed. Each decision you make antici- pates conditions you may encounter on your journey.

Similarly, when carving an intentional career path, it takes preparation and energy. If all your spoons are used up fulfilling daily commitments, you don't have any to devote to your career refinement efforts. To free up spoons for that purpose, step back and take a 360-degree view of your life. List out the different components that make up your overall well-being. This includes your physical health, mental health, confidence, community support, intimacy, connection, spirit, fun, adventure, and creativity. Assess how you are doing and investing currently in each of these areas as your baseline.

Next, document what success looks like for you in each area, noting the gap between where you are and where you want to be. Then, outline the steps required to close each gap, including the level of effort and your willingness to take the actions required.

With this inventory made, determine areas of highest priority to spend your spoons on first. When Jennifer, the VP of Engineering who had been at her company for more than twenty years and was struggling to make a change to a more fulfilling job, did this, she discovered the need to prioritize her mental health before anything else. After seeking support for mild depression, her energy increased, bringing within reach her ability to both refine her current situation and secure a new role.

To make the professional changes you desire, diverting time from your workday—and/or weekend—to devote to big-picture thinking is a must. If time feels in short supply, you may need to track where it is currently going to discover opportunities to reallocate some to higher leverage activities. Do this and you'll discover that you can be more intentional about how you spend your spoons.

Short-circuit your suffering

As humans, we naturally tend to repeat specific behaviors, some of which benefit us while others do not. One way to lower the stress in your work life is to train yourself to notice negative behavior patterns and the events that trigger them. Then you can focus on reducing the amount and the intensity of their negative impact. Often, this approach is more practical than trying to eliminate the cycle of behavior altogether.

Jessica experienced a periodic, repeating pattern she called her "death spiral," the vortex of strong feelings that surfaced when facing a challenging assignment at work. The phenomenon tended to take Jessica off her game for several days at a time, and she wanted to eliminate it altogether. Whenever she came to see me in the throes of a spiral, Jessica felt unsure how to navigate it, like it was happening to her for the first time. My job in these situations was to remind her of her resilience. I helped her recognize the natural rhythm of her energy pattern so she could work with it, not against it.

Typically, Jessica's downward spiral was triggered by a daunting request from senior leadership, sparking a sense of being overwhelmed and a loss of focus on tasks at hand. As time passed and she procrastinated, Jessica's sense of "the sky is falling" made it hard for her to get even basic things done. Finally, with the deadline looming, she would draft a rough outline and approach to meet the request, working step by step. After toiling down to the wire to prepare her materials, she would present her findings. Inevitably, Jessica would receive accolades for her insightful, high-quality perspective and then feel on top of the world.

For Jessica, a challenging request from senior leadership can trigger a physical sensation in her chest, like she can't breathe. With coaching, she learned to notice that visceral feeling and redirect her attention to actions that reduce her panic and increase her chance for success. For her, drafting a rough plan for a project allows her to breathe again. It flips the switch on her internal chaos, revealing a path forward, and bringing her back to her emotional center. Although it does not eliminate the difficult emotions, it reduces their frequency, duration, and intensity, giving her back a sense of control while conserving her energy.

Whether or not you experience a recurring spiral like Jessica's, or a different cycle of behavior, your fervent desire may be to stop experiencing the negative pattern. However, that may not be practical, as some behaviors are deeply seated and hard to fully eliminate. Rather, a pragmatic approach is to learn to recognize the cycle when it starts and redirect your attention to defuse its negative effects.

Recognizing what provokes your own downward spiral is key—it's typically a body sensation. You may notice pressure in your chest, hair standing up on the back of your neck, or a ball in the pit of your stomach. Whatever it is, pay attention to it, because it is the cue you need to redirect your focus.

Next, play through the natural rhythm of what happens when you experience the trigger. What do you do first, and how do you feel? What do you do next? What brings on the suffering, and what alleviates it? Write down the pattern so you can recognize its shape and where the opportunities are. Finally, notice what brings you up and out of the pattern. What tightens the circle to make it take less steps, time, and suffering to navigate? With awareness and practice, you can reduce the impact these episodes have on you. The internal dialogue can be, "Oh, I'm doing it again. When I feel the pressure in my chest, I direct my attention *here* and do *this.*"

Release energy tied up in seeming career missteps

Your career is not a straight upward trajectory but rather is filled with ups and downs. Career hiccups can distract you, shifting your attention to what happened in your past instead of what is possible in your present and future. Left unchecked, these preoccupations—difficult feelings, hard emotions, angst, and regret—interfere with achieving your goals. To access your finest work, you need to remove these obstacles from your path.

When you find yourself obsessing about a past situation and unable to let it go, there are typically two reasons: 1) There is a kernel of truth in it, something to learn that you have not allowed yourself to fully see or accept, and/ or 2) You have unfinished business. To resolve the inner conflict, find the lesson, learn from the experience, and put the wisdom you gain to use. Also, figure out the part you played in the situation and make peace with your actions.

Anne found herself thinking compulsively about a member of a neighboring work group who was giving her team grief. With coaching, she realized that although the colleague's behavior irritated her, she was most frustrated that her vision of stellar interdepartmental collaboration was going unrealized. Once connected with the real issue, Anne was able to put her exasperation into its proper place, focusing instead on how to propel her vision into being. This involved taking that perspective to her challenging colleague's department head and partnering with him to bring it to life.

In addition, Anne felt guilty about having raised her voice with the colleague who frustrated her. After our meeting, she called him to apologize for her tone, feeling an immediate sense of relief. With these two steps taken, Anne's suffering ebbed, and she was able to turn her attention elsewhere.

There are a variety of ways to release pent-up energy—journaling, talking with a therapist, adopting Julia Cameron's Morning Pages practice, meditating, and exercising are a few examples. Find outlets to express yourself, in formats and amounts that suit you, and apply them on an on-going basis. If you, like Anne, feel mired in negative feelings about a past—or current—career episode, consider journaling answers to reflective questions such as these:

1. What career misstep am I holding onto?
2. What feels bad or charged for me about this experience?
3. What is this situation teaching me? What is the learning opportunity?
4. How can I incorporate this learning into my go-forward plan?
5. If I feel at fault for my part in this episode, what do I need to take care of with myself and others to forgive myself to move on to what I truly want?
6. What do I need to do to stop reliving this experience and distracting myself from moving forward professionally?
7. What does letting go of the pain of experience do for me? What does it make room for in my life?

Consider repeating the reflection for any seeming career mistakes, beginning with the most preoccupying one. The point is to stop berating yourself, redirecting your attention to the lessons that can inform your way forward. These learnings may bring to your attention qualities you want more of—or less of—in your next professional chapter.

For example, you may find that in the future you desire:

- better alignment with the mission or goals of the company
- improved partnership with neighboring teams
- a strong network with other leaders to better insulate you should a particular executive leave or a reorganization occur
- a narrower scope of job duties to allow you to focus your charter
- firmer boundaries about how you spend your time at work
- more independence, perhaps with a more flexible work arrangement

Reframing your career mishaps as steps on the path to your finest work is healing and reveals a sense of progression over time. Your past missteps—and successes—have led you to this moment, where you are uniquely equipped for your next great thing. The experiences that have scarred you allow you to evolve ever closer to the work environment and professional contribution that best suits you and brings out your best.

The fastest way to turn a career misstep from a liability into a strength is to identify the lesson in it. The longer it takes to receive the message, the more you suffer. It stands to reason, then, that the opposite is also true—the faster you learn the gift of a challenging experience, the more quickly you can move on to a more fulfilling one.

BABY STEPS YIELD TRANSFORMATIVE RESULTS

When burned out, you must take steps to restore your energy and rebuild your stamina to operate at your highest level. Though this concept may be easy to grasp on an intellectual level, it can feel harder to put into practice. However, if you don't take exhaustion seriously, you may find the decision ultimately gets made for you. You may experience a significant health setback or some other calamity that forces your hand. The invitation is to get in front of this dynamic, not in a grinding, be-more-disciplined manner, but in a softer, organic, work-smarter-not-harder way.

Jeff's journey to regain a sense of well-being took shape over time. After hiring me to coach him, he cut back on his obligations outside of work, including leaving a committee that had been a drain on his energy for years. He renegotiated some project deadlines and timeframes and reduced involvement on others. After examining where time was going, he gained back several hours per week by ceasing to attend some lower priority meetings and sending proxies to others.

Jeff also empowered his team to take on projects that didn't require his personal involvement, except at a high level, to ensure things were on track. He improved feedback loops to make sure he remained connected, up to speed, and able to act on issues before they blew up. By changing his orientation from being a *doer* to serving as a *coach-leader*, Jeff freed up his own time and attention while helping employees engage and truly step into their potential. Jeff also worked on forgiving himself for past mistakes, dropping baggage that no longer served him to make room for more of what he desired: a sense of peace and optimism.

These changes helped Jeff make room to take care of himself. He prioritized outstanding medical appointments and health issues, including completing past due medical tests. He also started seeing a therapist to deal with sadness and despair that had descended during the pandemic. Jeff upgraded his diet to include whole foods, with time-saving habits that made it easier to make good nutritional choices. He optimized sleep habits to improve the quality of his rest and slowly embedded light exercise into his routine, selecting activities he liked. Finally, Jeff made fun a regular part of life, returning to an enjoyable hobby and spending more time playing with family and friends.

The good news is that it's possible to navigate this. It requires you to recognize when you are running on empty and reach out for help from friends, family, and professionals as needed. If you find yourself feeling low, please don't go it alone—reach out for assistance. A therapist can be an excellent place to start. Beyond that, seeking a coach or accountability buddy can help you return to a place of equilibrium and move you toward your finest work.

5. TAKE IMPERFECT ACTION

From Feeling Paralyzed to Empowered and Evolving

THE TRAP: FIXATED ON DOING THINGS RIGHT

Once again, Lina wrote the email to her former colleague but found herself unable to hit "send." Feeling uncertain about how to frame her ask, she hesitated, putting off the request for help acquiring a job at his company. Why the hesitation? She doubted her message was clear and compelling enough to be taken seriously.

Unsure of her approach, Lina turned her attention to an overflowing inbox where she could add immediate value and gain a sense of satisfaction. That dopamine hit would give her enough to skate through the day. She would leave the proactive outreach for another time.

In quiet moments, Lina found herself feeling overwhelmed and filled with dread. Fearing she only had one shot at asking her connection for help, she didn't want to blow it! How could she maximize her chance for success?

She didn't know and didn't have the time to find out. What she really needed to do, she told herself, was set aside a whole Saturday to update her resume. Lina penciled the task into her calendar for a day two weeks in the future. However, when that day arrived, she found ways to distract herself so that by the time she could focus, the day was almost gone. Yet again she had kicked the can down the road.

A few weeks later, while doom scrolling late at night, Lina discovered that the job she had been targeting at her colleague's company had been filled. A sense of hopelessness washed over her. She wondered if she would *ever* get out of her current situation and into something better!

Six months passed. Her situation unchanged, Lina hired me to help her get out of her own way. Even then she avoided scheduling her first session because she wanted to be truly ready to get the most out of the coaching experience. She cited work projects to clear off her plate and a desire to spend time with my materials before beginning her sessions. However, given her schedule and fractured attention, her projects inevitably extended beyond their original scope. She failed to find the time to feel 100 percent ready to take advantage of the assistance coaching could provide her.

Lina was suffering from the fourth trap I see leaders fall into: fixated on doing things right. If you feel like you are consistently not making progress on your personal career priorities, you too may be suffering from analysis paralysis. To overcome this, you need to become a professional experimenter and practice taking imperfect action. Only then can you relax the grip on your own high standards and build a sense of momentum toward a better career.

REORIENT YOUR ATTENTION FROM YOUR *DOING* TO YOUR *BEING*

When you prioritize "doing things right," energetically everything grinds to a halt. In this state, it can be challenging to make progress of any kind toward your career ambitions. Because the stakes feel so high, you may avoid advocating for what you want. Especially when you haven't done enough research, or don't have all the answers, or don't want to look uninformed, you can feel internal resistance to taking action.

As a result, even if you long for a new job, you may avoid launching your search and instead endlessly rework your resume. You may avoid discussing a new role with your boss until your current projects are completed. You may shelve networking opportunities until you feel prepared or delay chances to explore new relationships and career arenas. Since you never feel ready, these activities get delayed over and over. Or, you might do as I did and focus on the *transaction* as opposed to the *transformational* opportunities in front of you.

After years of effort and two failed attempts, acquiring my Master Certified Coach Credential (MCC) seemed out of reach. Within five minutes of sharing the context with my newest mentor coach, Janet, she announced the reason I was failing: "You're trying too hard. Master coaching is about surrender."

Her words nearly knocked me over. I had sensed I was holding on too tight; however, it had never occurred to me that the path to achieving my goal was to let go, release my laser focus on reaching the summit, and turn my attention instead to the journey of climbing the mountain.

To date I had spent countless hours wondering what I was *doing wrong* and what I needed to *fix* to achieve my goal. I was preparing for a test I wanted to ace. Janet's invitation to redirect my attention from passing the exam to upgrading my coaching presence was powerful. Her words revealed a path forward, shifting my focus and enabling me to notice things that had been invisible to me before.

Around the same time, I received a bouquet of flowers from Pam, my business coach at the time, with a card that I still keep on my desk, years later. It says, "*No external 'no', can match the power of an internal YES.*"

What a concept! I began to see that there was a life lesson to learn, much deeper than any I had imagined. It was humbling to realize I had been pursuing this designation as proof of my abilities instead of realizing that *I* alone could approve of *myself*. That inner approval was more powerful than any external achievement, and surrendering was a key component.

Until then, I had seriously considered giving up my goal. Perhaps the lesson was that I didn't need to prove to anyone that I was good at my craft? I marinated in that thought for a while. However, a question kept resurfacing for me. Perhaps there was an opportunity to not only become a more skilled practitioner but also a more evolved human being? This curiosity sustained me during dark moments and gave me the energy to continue.

For me, it took Janet and Pam's words together to redirect my focus from the quality of my *doing* to that of my *being*.

Slowly, over time, I took a deep breath and relaxed. All the training I had undertaken to learn to coach others, I applied to myself. I detached from the outcome of achieving the credential. I began to notice more opportunities to help my clients tune into themselves. My new mindset helped me absorb lessons from my mentor coaches and assessors with more openness. Gradually, this led to transformational shifts in my coaching, and ultimately to me acquiring my Master Coaching Credential.

Endeavoring to make a change professionally provides the opening to pay attention on a deeper level to what is going on inside of you. The real gains take place when you fall in love with the journey and what the experience is trying to teach you. Then you can take concerted action, one step at a time, to truly unlock your next level, and do your finest work.

CHANGE YOUR RUBRIC FOR SUCCESS

At the relentless pace of change and uncertainty that defines modern life, trying to "do things right" is a path to futility, and an exhausting way to live. What a game-changer—and competitive advantage—to realize that you can experiment instead, trying things, and if they don't work, trying something else! It's a competitive advantage to take imperfect action because it gets you ahead of those plagued by perfectionism.

Career transformation happens gradually. You facilitate positive change by opening your mind, body, and spirit to the journey and what it can teach you. You keep your North Star top of mind while taking small, calculated risks to make progress toward your goals. Observing the results of your efforts as you go, you refine your approach to draw ever closer to your ideal situation. Transformation is an evolution, not a one-shot deal.

"To be a successful entrepreneur, you need to think of yourself as a professional experimenter. The beliefs you hold are just assumptions." Sitting in the audience at the Haas School of Business' Women in Leadership conference years ago, I didn't expect to completely rewire my belief system about change. However, IndieGoGo co-founder Danae Ringelmann's words galvanized me. Although her share was focused on entrepreneurship, the wisdom rings true for the broader context of career transformation.

Only by releasing the fixation on "making the right choice" and "taking the right steps" do we gain the ability to achieve meaningful change. Like a scientist, we hold loosely to our assumptions, secure in what we are optimizing for, while remaining agile about the route to the results. If something doesn't pan out as we hoped it would, we frame a new approach and continue investigating. We harness resources to support our queries, following the bread-crumbs to gradually move toward our desired destination.

What might this look like? Instead of endlessly retooling your resume, hire a resume writer to pull you through the process. Or timebox yourself to update the document to be "good enough" so you can begin networking with people in a position to help you. In your current role (if you have one), carve out time one-on-one with your boss to discuss your career development. Articulate what you want based on what you know now, and gain insight on how to fill the gaps between where you are and where you want to be.

If you want to grow your influence with your colleagues, schedule short quarterly one-on-ones with peers to deepen those relationships. Ask open-ended questions and then co-design a mutually productive agenda for future sessions. When contacting people for informational interviews, draft a short list of open-ended, intentional questions to elicit what you need to know to make an informed decision about your path. With each small action, observe what works and adjust your methods to incorporate lessons learned. The effect over time is a spiraling upward toward more of what you want and away from what you don't.

When the choke hold of requiring everything to be "all figured out" before acting takes its grip, it can be hard to shake free. To counteract this, you must lower the stakes to make each thing you do matter less, taking incremental actions toward your goal.

LOWER THE STAKES

After learning that avoiding scheduling appointments with me mirrored what she wanted to change about her career approach, Lina finally began her coaching. Over a series of sessions, she surprised herself by confirming what she really wanted—a career change. In essence, the roles she was applying for felt too much like the one she wanted to leave. It turned out that her ladder was up against the wrong wall.

Realizing that she wanted to move in a new direction terrified her. Lina's risk-averse nature resisted the effort and courage such a change would take. As she considered two possible fields, our work focused on lowering the stakes for her to explore these options without commitment. We engaged her curiosity while preparing her for the exploration process. For Lina, this meant crafting a script for informational interviews and making introductions to those in positions that appealed to her. By having a blueprint to follow and a clear purpose for networking, she lowered her anxiety.

What we *didn't* do was turn our attention to her personal brand or job search—it would have been premature to undertake those tasks. Rather, Lina navigated her way forward to career clarity one conversation at a time. She asked open-ended questions to get the other person talking. As she engaged with others to explore what they did and how they got there, Lina started to relax. People were happy to help, eager to share about their line of work and advise on what they had learned along the way. Lina asked and was introduced to others who contributed to her body of knowledge about the two career options she had under examination. Ultimately, one career direction emerged over the other as her choice.

Delighted to feel grounded about her path forward, Lina focused on reducing the barriers to entering her new, chosen field. She enrolled in a certification program to learn the required skills and to hang out with professionals who were doing the work, beginning to "look the part" for the new role she was now committed to.

At work, she noticed opportunities to volunteer for projects that reinforced what she was learning in the certification program. Although her ultimate plan was to leave her employer for a new company, she investigated whether she could first move internally to her new line of work. She explored that option with her boss and then with Human Resources.

Meanwhile, she hired out the updates of her resume and LinkedIn profile, finding it more efficient to be pulled through the process than doing it herself. The writer refined her career story to make a compelling case for her chosen target. As the narrative took shape, Lina helped the writer describe not only where she'd come from but also where she was headed.

Lina also procured a new professional headshot to bring her inner experience of who she was becoming into the image she projected outwardly to others. We named the headshot "Lina 2.0," a powerful metaphor to return to whenever she felt the uncertainty and paralysis that was her temperamental tendency. She found the new photo to be a beacon for her new chapter and gazed at it whenever she needed a dose of courage.

As her professional experiments continued and her certification neared completion, Lina was tapped for a project that aligned with her new direction. Over the next six months, she worked diligently on the new assignment—no small feat as it came on top of the obligations of her current role. However, she was able to hold both sets of job duties because it was a means to an end. Provided she performed well, the extra project was a clear pathway to a role doing that type of work exclusively. It was a concrete accomplishment she could share with prospective employers as an example of the work she was now doing.

As the assignment wound down, Lina reached out to the former colleague she had previously avoided emailing to discuss her next chapter. Through the years they had enjoyed a strong relationship, and he was thrilled to hear of her new direction. As Lina described her current project, he began proactively searching for a place for her in his company. At the same time, she received an invitation to join the team she had completed the project for full-time. Within a short time, Lina had two offers to choose from, both focused on her new path.

PRACTICES AND TACTICS

Focusing on taking imperfect action is a liberating paradigm. As a professional experimenter, you don't have to figure everything out up front to gain fulfilling, satisfying work! With your non-negotiables in hand, you can loosely hold positions and perspectives, secure in the awareness that you are drawing ever closer to your ideal career. You can feel free to miss the mark, achieve partial wins, and change course along the way.

Experimentation enables an ever-evolving upward spiral into new chapters of your finest work. The goal is to become more *nimble*, to be able to cover more ground with less effort, adapting easily to what you are learning about yourself and your intended path. Rather than be immobilized by a fear of making mistakes, you can proceed while stepping lightly, with a sense of detachment. These practices and tactics partner well with the free bonus tools you can access at **www.yourfinestwork.com**.

Follow the CLEAR process

CLEAR stands for Clarify - Learn - Evaluate - Act - Refine. I created this decision-making process to guide executives through resolving any strategic question or issue they care about. It is simple and encourages imperfect action. You can apply it to refining your career trajectory, preparing for an important presentation, or anything in between. Below is a short description of each step.

Step 1 - Clarify

Name the question or problem you are trying to answer or solve. How will you know you have solved or answered it well? Focus your attention on how you will measure a successful outcome. If you rush this step, you risk not solving the right problem. Characterize the gap between where you are now and where you want to be.

Step 2 - Learn

Brainstorm a set of alternatives for bridging the gap. What ideas surface? What options exist? Prioritize those you have the most enthusiasm for—even if they feel out of reach right now—selecting two or three to evaluate first. Compare that set of options against your requirements to assess their likely fit. Craft and run a set of small experiments as needed to answer questions you have. Be curious, reaching out to others to gain any missing information. As needed, return to your list of ideas to assess more options until you feel satisfied.

Step 3 - Evaluate

Compare potential paths you are considering. Where is your best fit, given what you have learned? Confirm your choice or revisit the learning step until you can. One of three outcomes typically occurs:

1. A clear winner for the path to take emerges.
2. Multiple pathways appear to be the best fits, and you decide to pursue them simultaneously or sequentially.
3. None emerge as the right path, but a new option appears that does.

Step 4 - Act

Based on which outcome comes from the prior step, construct a rough plan for moving forward, mapping out your implementation strategy. Determine what needs to be done and prioritize your action steps. Decide what you will do, in what sequence, with the goal of getting to "good enough." Create and implement the solution, harnessing assistance from others as needed.

Step 5 - Refine

Make micro-adjustments to incorporate lessons learned from implementation. Solicit feedback from others to inform these tweaks, measuring your progress against what you set out to do originally. Over time, revisit the steps of the CLEAR process to improve your results.

Focus on getting to "good enough"

Arriving where you are in your career today may have involved setting high expectations and being unwilling to settle for anything less than fully meeting them. However, over time, those expectations can become so burdensome that an unwillingness to fail (perfectionism) takes over and you end up frozen in place. If you tend to fall prey to an overly analytical approach, know that you are not alone. To break that pattern, focus on ways to temper your expectations, making them realistically match the circumstances and resources at your disposal.

A good way to do this is to ask yourself, What does "good enough" look like for now for this task? This can be your go-to phrase for most projects. Embracing the "good enough" mindset does not imply putting out shoddy work; rather, it is an intentional evaluation of how much effort is needed to get something over the finish line.

Here are a few examples of this concept in action.

Instead of: Continuing to stew on your professional story before launching your job search

Do this: Get a draft out to your close-in connections and get some feedback, or conduct a few informational interviews and ask them for some input on how best to position yourself for the role you seek.

Instead of: Polishing up a document so it reads well

Do this: Roughly sketch a few conceptual ideas out on paper or a whiteboard and bring your team in to discuss and refine.

Instead of: Suffering over an article or social media post's wording

Do this: Set a timer to limit your effort and then put it out in the world and see how it resonates with your audience, learning from it what to do next.

The spirit of "good enough" involves framing projects in phases or milestones, taking a staircase approach, and integrating learnings over time. Instead of striving for perfection, consider embracing incremental improvement through drafting, iterating, and editing your way to quality outcomes. Establish processes for refinement, such as ongoing feedback loops. These approaches allow you and your team to take more risks and surface more innovative ideas, feeling safe to experiment. Your aim: to perform tasks in a way to meet a minimum level of completeness so that you can move on energetically, refining things over time as needed.

Cultivate your curiosity with open-ended questions

I had a chance to interview award-winning journalist and podcast host Tess Vigeland shortly after she left a high-profile career and wrote her first book, *Leap: Leaving a Job With no Plan B to Find the Career and Life You Really Want,* Harmony (August 25, 2015). Petrified and without a concrete plan for her next professional move, Tess likened the ups and downs to a roller coaster. Some days she felt ecstatic; on others she could barely get out of bed, thinking she had made the biggest mistake of her life by leaving her job as the national broadcast news anchor for Marketplace Money. Despite the highs and lows, she felt fortunate to have taken the leap instead of continuing to rotate around in circles in her job.

Tess used her curiosity to figure out her path forward. While researching the book that inspired her own leap, she interviewed eighty people, asking open-ended questions to learn their stories and strategies for change. She came to realize that a career is not a straight line but an Etch A Sketch, where you can make an intricate image and then, when tired of that particular picture, shake it up to produce a blank canvas upon which to create a new one. This playful metaphor gave her courage as she traveled extensively throughout Southeast Asia to learn how to live a happier, healthier life. Returning to the USA with a fresh perspective, she began the next phase of her career.

Whether you are contemplating a major or minor career pivot, cultivating curiosity helps you successfully navigate the chasm between where you are and where you want to be. Entering exploratory conversations with an open mind and thoughtful questions helps you gain the knowledge you seek. In our complex world, it is impossible to know everything; asking targeted questions and listening actively to the answers makes the way forward feel actionable and light.

Whether you are planning for a one-on-one with your boss, a networking meeting with a colleague, or conducting an informational interview to explore a new field, preparing discerning, open-ended questions helps you maximize the opportunity. It is easy to squander face time with someone in a position to help you. Instead, identify in advance what you want to learn and craft questions designed to procure that outcome.

For informational interviews exploring a new job or career direction, the questions stem from your non-negotiables. Don't waste time discussing how the person got into their role or what their company does (but study those things ahead of time). Rather, frame questions to get to the bottom of how their day-to-day reality matches—or doesn't match—the future situation you would like for yourself. For example, if you enjoy facilitating cross-functional alignment, ask the person to provide examples of that skillset in action.

When navigating discussions with your boss to explore advancement opportunities, be transparent and descriptive about where you want more experience, and explore how best to access it. In one-on-one networking sessions with peers to build stronger relationships, share the type of work you specialize in and enjoy. Probe where those abilities are most likely to help your colleagues succeed.

Open-ended questions are inquiries that cannot be answered with a yes or a no. Designed to get the other person talking, they typically begin with "how" or "what," "tell me about a time," "explain," or "describe." They allow the receiver to immediately jump into sharing mode. For example, when negotiating the terms of an interesting job offer, you might say, "I'm looking for an overall compensation package in the $X to $Y range. How can we get there?" This phraseology engenders a sense of two people problem-solving together, sitting on the same side of the table with their sleeves rolled up. The problem can be solved a variety of ways (in this case, by increasing the base salary, adding to the bonus, including equity, upping the benefits package, bumping up the role level and associated pay grade, etc.)—that is part of the dance back and forth. The open-ended framing invites the dance to reach an outcome that serves both parties in a collegial way.

When in a meeting without time to prepare or when you are taken by surprise, use open-ended questions to facilitate a productive outcome. "I'm noticing that we are talking a lot about X; however, at the start of this meeting we said we were here to talk about Y. How shall we handle this?" Or "I'm noticing that people are checking their phones and the energy seems low. What do we want to do about this?" This format instantly forms a bridge between you and others, inviting them to engage and create a path forward with you.

After asking an open-ended question, *be silent.* Even if it feels awkward and lasts for a bit longer than you feel comfortable, keep your mouth shut. In this case, silence is a good thing; it means people are thinking. You've asked a solid question; now allow others to take their time with the answer. The quality of the interchange improves when you do.

Brainstorm options for moving forward

Josh felt unsure about his next professional move but craved a change. He'd worked as a software engineer and web designer. Now, he felt unsure whether he wanted to continue along one of those paths or follow a new direction. Reviewing his non-negotiables, Josh prioritized fun and play, contributing to a meaningful cause, and building things from the ground up. He also prioritized having clear expectations and purpose from his employer, control over his work environment, a sense of orderliness, and regular recognition for his efforts. In his personal life, he enjoyed yoga, tiny homes, travel, movies, sports, teaching, and being outside. He felt passionate about technology and the small group of software developers he regularly gathered with to kick around ideas for new startups.

Josh longed for fresh ways to apply his skills and interests in his career. So we compiled a list of options to explore. As we brainstormed, we walked through what he enjoyed and valued, careful not to limit ourselves by feasibility concerns at this point in the process. Here is the list we came up with, in no particular order:

- screenwriter
- boot camp creator for aspiring software engineers
- CEO of his own startup—being the ringleader with people he has worked with in the past
- YouTube personality, making videos
- podcaster
- app developer
- something to do with climate change
- motivational speaker
- website designer—or building software to help consulting businesses operate and grow
- personal training, owning a gym, personal coach, or instructor— helping people become athletes
- journalist/some kind of writer—technical writer, magazines, blog writer, novelist
- sports announcer
- sports partnerships developer
- sports ambassador
- community organizer—convening people together for a purpose
- something with chemistry—product development,

chemistry kits for kids, making chemistry easy for kids to learn

- online instructor for courses that teach people how to do things
- network/strategic partnerships development
- sound design
- architecture
- systems architecture
- innovation—i.e., head an innovation lab
- scrum master leading agile development
- systems or business analyst
- actor
- facilitating playfulness in the workplace—comedian/ improv specialist, helping businesspeople and teams learn improv
- tour designer and/or guide for adventure travel
- yoga instructor, meditation teacher and/or massage therapist
- retreat center owner
- owner of a co-working space—combo artist enclave /performance venue
- operator for a kids' summer/spring break/after school camp
- run a theater program
- work for/mentor startups in an accelerator environment
- interim CTO for startups
- nutritionist

Having this list in hand filled Josh with enthusiasm. He now had ideas to start to investigate and picked some immediate favorites to explore first. He held onto the possibility that some options could coexist in a portfolio career, like executive coach Larry enjoyed. Larry split his time between leading a business school's career center, coaching executives at a top technology company, and teaching graphic design at a local art college. Josh even entertained the option of continuing down his current path for his day job and starting a side hustle.

If you would like to explore some potential options for your next professional move, consider journaling answers to the following questions. Suspend feasibility for the moment. For now, follow your energy without regard for practicality. Assume you have the experience and training needed for any option that appeals to you.

Here are the prompts:

- What career options have you previously thought of?
- What did you want to be when you grew up?
- What do your loved ones think you are well suited for?
- Review your professional and personal interests. What fields or roles are these associated with?
- Walk through the skills that come easily to you and that you enjoy. What career arenas do these talents make you think of?
- Reflect on who you admire professionally. What career arenas do they work in that appeal to you?
- If you have taken any career assessments, pull out any career options that resonate from them.

- If a recruiter has presented a job that interested you, add that type of role.
- Conduct a few quick job listing searches using keywords from your interests, competency areas, and skills, finding a small handful of interesting roles (even if you don't meet all the requirements).
- If you have interviewed for jobs in the past year that appeal to you, add those roles.

A list of potential pathways will emerge, including new ideas as well as old ones. Then you can start exploring and evaluating.

Engage your intuition with the quick and dirty draft

Priya rushed into our coaching session visibly flustered. There was never enough time in the day! A conscientious leader of a large engineering organization, she found herself consumed by the responsibilities that came with the job. The latest demand was to write performance reviews for herself and her team. She was already behind on the task, with the deadline looming. She dreaded the long hours to complete this task but resigned herself to doing so; not only was it compulsory, but taking care of her people was one of her highest priorities.

Overall, Priya came to coaching wanting to reduce her stress, increase her strategic influence, and become more productive. With more work to do than time to do it, diving too deep into the details was not feasible. Although a detail-oriented style of management had served her well at an earlier stage of her career, this playbook no longer worked with her executive role and global charter.

As I listened to Priya gripe about the performance reviews, I could imagine her internal tape recorder playing—"Here we go again, just the latest hard thing on the never-ending path of hard things. Where is the time going to come from to tackle this well?"

What we did next changed her life. We challenged her internal recording.

"What makes performance review writing hard?" I asked.

Priya described her process, which involved several detailed steps. For each employee, she reread last year's content, paged through the calendar, then scoured team roadmaps and progress reports to make sure she was comprehensive. Only then did she distill and translate her notes into the performance review software. I felt tired just hearing about her process!

Together we considered whether there was another, easier way to complete the reviews. She had more than ten to write in a very short time. How could she make the process less taxing?

We designed a simple method for her to experiment with. First, she would just sit and concentrate on the person being reviewed. Then she would engage her intuition and make some notes. With this approach, Priya could formulate a high-level picture of the person's key accomplishments, strengths, and areas for improvement from the past year. She would rely on what was top of mind to produce a quick and dirty draft, and then move on to the next person, repeating the same process. Once she had completed a first pass through all employees, she would quickly review the prior year's data to spot check her work.

Priya was skeptical. It seemed so easy! However, reducing her workload and effort was a high priority, so she took on the challenge.

The next time I saw her, she wore a bright smile, sharing her surprise at having been able to complete the reviews with relative ease. After penning drafts guided by her intuition, Priya found that when reviewing the backup materials, she had caught the most important points. Through this experience, Priya learned that she could trust her gut to surface the most important details. She considered where else she could apply this method to reduce her effort without sacrificing quality.

Over time, embracing the quick and dirty draft method to complete various tasks became a regular practice for Priya. It helped reorient her attention from exclusively considering data and analysis to paying attention to her inner knowing. Changing her focus from being thorough and avoiding mistakes to capturing the most important nuggets paid off in multiple ways. With practice, Priya began to rely on her gut more and more, reducing her stress while growing her throughput, influence, and impact.

The intuitive first draft accomplishes two goals at once: 1) it makes the task you are completing easier and 2) helps you learn to trust yourself. The best news is that it can be applied to pretty much any situation. Using this powerful technique can help you author a presentation, craft a product roadmap, strategize the approach to a complex project, write a keynote speech, pre-plan a challenging conversation, draft a book chapter, outline your elevator pitch, or prepare for a job interview, to name a few possibilities.

A high-level draft helps you tease out your main points without getting mired in the details. It gives you something to work with and refine over time, bringing others in to support you as needed. You may find that in many cases the draft is all that is required! Use it and you'll cover more ground toward your goals with less effort.

STEADY YOURSELF IN UNCERTAINTY

Taking imperfect action is by nature imperfect. The welcome surprise is that you and the situations you face are much more resilient than you think. You drop a ball, and even if it breaks, you can recover. Embracing failure and recovering quickly are skills you can learn.

When you berate yourself for perceived or actual mistakes, notice your self-talk. Then, consciously shift it to build yourself up instead of tearing yourself down. When you talk to yourself kindly, your results change. Consistent, positive self-talk starts a chain reaction. It shifts your feelings, which then change your belief systems, which modifies your actions, which ultimately transform your outcomes. It takes consistency but is worth the effort.

Bottom line: think of career missteps as failing up. The next time you experience a misstep, mistake, or misunderstanding, remember to take a deep breath, remain calm, and see the opportunity to lead and learn. Your successes and your mistakes make you who you are and lead to your next big opportunity when you keep putting one foot in front of the other.

When a ship is tossed about in a storm, it can be tempting to focus on the individual waves pummeling it. To reduce disorientation, the captain focuses on the horizon. This same logic holds when you are skippering your career. Expand your view and focus on *your* personal horizon line to steer toward more of what you want and less of what you don't, over time.

With your North Star guiding you, you have enough information to travel from where you are to where you want to be. The journey is paved with experiments, observations, and course corrections. You navigate it by taking one imperfect action at a time, letting your curiosity guide you. Though you can't see it at first, your path will become clear as you travel toward your personal horizon. When you let go of the need to know and the need to "do things right," the way forward gradually becomes visible, enabling you to access your finest work.

6. FINE-TUNE
YOUR POWERS OF
OBSERVATION

From Attending to Tasks to Attending to Energy

THE TRAP: A NARROW, TRANSACTIONAL FOCUS

Ramesh was flabbergasted to learn that his stakeholders found him to be a sub-optimal partner. As we reviewed the feedback from the 360 review I had conducted on his behalf, he gasped in disbelief. Ramesh worked alongside a cross-functional array of colleagues every day to drive the company's highest-profile, multi-million-dollar technology project. He found it difficult to hear that he was doing anything other than hitting it out of the park. Ramesh felt misunderstood and demoralized. This feedback was certainly going to get in the way of the promotion he was working toward!

The report revealed that Ramesh's stakeholders did not feel adequately listened to; instead, they noticed that he came to meetings intent on his agenda. Rather than anticipate and proactively address their concerns, he waited for others to raise them. When they did, he tended to act defensively, make excuses, and imply he was on top of things when he truly wasn't. The result? His partners felt a lack of collaboration, a sense of distrust, and misalignment.

In his attempt to balance scope creep with a firm budget and fixed timeline, Ramesh's communication style left others feeling like he was not an ideal partner. Hearing this news confused and embarrassed him, and he didn't know what to do about it.

Ramesh was suffering from the fifth trap I see leaders fall into—single-mindedness and a narrow, transactional focus. In his quest to execute on his job, he failed to notice the energy in the room when communicating with others. Instead, his attention was trained on *his* agenda, meeting *his* needs, and one-way communication from *him* to *them*. By focusing on being efficient, he was missing the mark—the intangibles of trust-building.

To rectify this, Ramesh needed to shift his attention to observing and listening deeply to those around him. He needed to fine-tune his powers of observation to take in more information and let that expanded data set inform how he navigated his daily interactions.

UNDERSTAND ENERGY EXCHANGE

When I listen to a leader like Ramesh in a coaching session, I pay attention to more than what he is saying. I'm observing him closely, noticing how he moves, the look in his eyes, and where he puts his hands. I take in the emotion that comes off him and the tone of his voice. This information blends naturally with the words he is saying and the agenda he has for our meeting. I am truly paying attention on multiple levels—to words spoken, body language, and energy. It is a powerful combination that gives me tools to help Ramesh, and other leaders like him, help themselves.

This energetic awareness is a valuable tool because it shows the path to a win-win outcome in any interaction. It reveals the information you need to drive any conversation to serve all stakeholders involved. Being able to listen and observe in this way is a skillset that if not already honed, can be learned. Over time, practicing these skills reduces your effort to achieve the outcomes you want—and which others need—across the hundreds of interactions you navigate daily.

Ramesh's 360 review revealed that he was listening one-dimensionally. When we began coaching, he was not aware that an additional way of paying attention existed. He had grown up in the company recognized for his ability to execute. To not take someone's comments at face value was a foreign concept to him. In fact, Ramesh had come to prioritize executing on time and on budget over everything else. He was known and commended for this—it was his personal brand, and he was proud of it.

However, as he advanced up the professional ladder, his execution skillset was no longer sufficient to address the nuanced communication cross-functional collaboration requires. An ambitious leader with an eye on continued advancement, the 360 feedback was a wake-up call, inviting him to pay attention in a new way. It confused him at first. As an engineer, Ramesh found that the message didn't immediately appeal to his logical, analytical mind.

Fortunately, he was so destabilized by the feedback that he was willing to experiment with new approaches. He was also a fundamentally kind, genial person who wanted to do an excellent job for his stakeholders. To that end, he was eager to practice new competencies but unaware of how to do so.

Over our next few sessions, Ramesh and I constructed a process that enabled him to tune into the energetic frequency of any meeting to define the *true* agenda. He learned that after sending out the meeting outline in advance, there was an opportunity to refine it with the people in the room. This way he was sure to cover the various aspects participants expected, immediately gaining buy-in that their needs would be met.

When expectations surfaced that he had not anticipated, he could 1) expand the agenda to include those pieces, or 2) tag them as excluded and identify how to address them separately. With the true meeting agenda now identified, Ramesh could facilitate the interaction with this as his guide, addressing both his needs and those of his constituents.

With practice, Ramesh learned to notice energy exchange in conversations and to address the unspoken. In fact, he became known as the technical leader who called out the "elephant in the room" when no one else was willing or able to. He asked open-ended questions based on what he observed. He considered all aspects of first-class delivery of technology solutions, including execution *and* stakeholder engagement. It was evident to his superiors and partners that he had learned and was using a new set of leadership skills. Ramesh was delighted to discover that by embodying these qualities, he could gain cross-functional alignment more quickly and reduce complexity for his team in their execution of important company initiatives.

TAKE THE COMPASSIONATE VIEW

Imagine you are in the final throes of preparing to deliver what you know will be a tough performance review for one of your employees. Although you have provided your direct report, Serena, bits of feedback previewing the review's contents, your intuition tells you she will feel broadsided. Serena is a tricky personality to manage and a member of the old guard you inherited when taking over the team a few years ago. She brings a sense of combativeness and defensiveness to each interaction, regardless of subject. Throughout the time you have managed her, you have worked hard to neither internalize nor reciprocate those behaviors. It has been challenging!

Although it hasn't happened yet, you can already imagine the flow of the review delivery conversation. You will each come into the session visibly neutral, and then as you share the feedback, Serena will grow increasingly frustrated and defensive. She will likely lash out and make statements about how the review doesn't seem fair. She might criticize your leadership, dispute the points of feedback, or make excuses for her behavior. The end of the meeting will not come fast enough, with Serena retreating to lick her wounds and disparage the process and your leadership to her colleagues. You will leave the meeting exhausted and relieved to have it behind you.

Based on your premonition, you resign yourself to the review delivery being a miserable experience that produces neither insights nor growth for either party but is something simply to survive. So you are surprised in our coaching session when we move *away* from how to phrase the feedback to Serena and, instead, move *toward* how to hold and manage the energy produced by the interaction.

We start by imagining being in Serena's shoes. We anticipate how she will likely feel arriving for her performance review delivered by a manager she doesn't mesh well with and who likely doesn't have a high opinion of her. From this vantage point, your steely resolve to endure the review starts to shift to a compassionate one. What can you do to make Serena feel safe and receptive to the feedback so she can have the best chance to learn from it?

As your body relaxes and the lens of your attention softens, you can now design an experience based not on minimizing your discomfort but rather one that holds the strong emotion that Serena is likely to feel and the sense of vulnerability the experience will create for her. With this new awareness, you can shape a safe container for the two of you to inhabit during and after the conversation. This will enable Serena to be able to process the feedback in an intentional, actionable way, on her own terms.

With your attention now squarely trained on energy, you design for Serena's metaphorical hair to be blown back by the feedback. You know how important Serena's job at the company is to her self-image. You decide to offer her the option to separate the review into two sessions, one to receive the feedback and one to respond to it. This choice puts Serena in the driver's seat, helping her regain a sense of control.

When the review takes place, Serena ultimately elects to split the conversation into two pieces. After walking through the feedback, you adjourn. A few days later you reconvene to discuss Serena's response to the review's contents. You ask open-ended questions to get her talking and pay attention to her responses. When she pauses, you reflect on what you hear her saying, mirroring Serena's words to confirm you heard her correctly. When she acknowledges that you have, you ask "What else?" to make sure she has the chance to share all her insights. You notice and speak to Serena's body language, inviting her to share more of what is going on internally, beyond what she is saying out loud.

Although the experience isn't pleasant for either of you, it douses the fire for Serena to be listened to in such a deep way. She can speak in a composed, thoughtful manner about where she finds the feedback to be spot on. She can point out where it feels out of alignment with how she sees herself. Together you identify a couple of areas to focus on going forward. You provide Serena with the tools she needs to be successful while meeting deadlines and improving collaboration with you and others. You both leave feeling heard and resolved on clear next steps to take in tandem.

By fine-tuning your powers of observation, you become conscious of the true factors at play, on multiple levels (words spoken, body language, and energy). You recognize what *you* need (to get the review delivered and have your message land), what *Serena* needs (to feel respected with the space to truly process the feedback), and what the *situation* warrants (a constructive, two-way

discussion to help Serena with her professional growth).
This multi-faceted awareness enables you to take informed,
intentional action to address all these components.

BECOME A NATURAL NOTICER

Strategic leaders tend to lean heavily on their thinking
mind when navigating the workday. As a result, it can be
easy to miss cues, especially energetic ones, related to
body language, tone of voice, and intent behind a spoken
message. Learning to pick up on these elements can yield
many benefits, the most obvious of which is solving the
right problem.

You may be a natural noticer, but if not, it is a skill you
can develop. Building awareness is a combination of three
centers of intelligence: mind/logical thinking, heart/spirit
recognition, and body/gut knowing. By growing the ability to
notice what is going on within and around you from all three of
these centers, you have a lot of data to inform your actions.

With these tools at your disposal, you can observe and
address the various dynamics at play. This includes what
you want and what others intend and are trying to make
happen with their words and actions. You can recognize
what your part of the problem is to solve and what is others'
work to do and not yours. Throughout each day, you can
telescope up to the macro view and back down to the micro
level to gain perspective.

Ashley came to our coaching session wanting to debrief
her recent interviews with a fintech startup entertaining her
for a CEO role. She had spent a full day with the leadership
team learning about the opportunity and communicating

her qualifications. She had diligently prepared and presented a 30-60-90-day plan to familiarize them with her intended approach. In her presentation, she mapped out how the company would establish market leadership while transforming itself into a well-run operation with a metrics-driven culture. As Ashley reviewed the slide deck with me and talked through her key points, it was clear that she had a strong strategy for leading growth for the company.

Noticing how I felt as I listened to her presentation, I asked, "How did the leaders in the room react?"

"It was a bit hard to tell," she replied. "The chief product officer (CPO) seemed a bit resistant. The board member really liked the reports section and asked for a copy of my slides."

I invited her to drill down on the CPO's reaction. What made him resistant? It mirrored how *I* felt as she walked through her slides, which were full of detailed operational instructions. When Ashley put herself in the CPO's shoes, she realized that it was a lot to take in—and a lot to change. Since it was different than the path currently being taken, it implied that the leadership team was on the wrong path. I was not surprised to hear that the CPO was hesitant!

Ashley is an extremely polished leader who displays finesse in the way she carries herself. Her presence and her slide deck revealed that she knows what she is doing and has experience leading a company through the steps required to scale. However, Ashley deprioritized the cue the CPO was giving her—the need to invite him in and bring him along.

Ashley's proposed approach involved significant effort in a new direction. She needed to help the team understand that although there was new ground to cover, she would meet them where they were. Together, they would learn from what was working already, and partner every step of the way to achieve the new vision. The opportunity was to communicate how they would do this *together*. They needn't be threatened by her candidacy; rather, she would be their partner and guide in achieving success, impact, and scale.

Missing this cue may or may not have been a deal breaker for this opportunity. However, now that she was aware of this dynamic, she could look for these types of openings in conversations in the future and tackle them head-on. Rather than feel bad about missing the cue this time, she could learn from it and tune into the frequency of the energy in future sessions.

PRACTICES AND TACTICS

Rather than train your attention on a single dimension when interacting with others, fine-tuning your powers of observation allows you to focus on multiple levels of information gathering at once. You can notice what is being said and not said, what you and others need, and what shifts are required to produce a mutually beneficial outcome. Your goal is to gain *insight*, helping you solve each problem more comprehensively versus simply treating a symptom of the problem. These practices and tactics pair well with the free bonus tools you can access at **www.yourfinestwork.com**.

Read the room

Many strategic leaders I coach aspire to have more influence and impact. At the same time, they have invested heavily in their technical abilities. Accustomed to being known for their awesomeness, they approach work using a common formula: personally figure out a problem; work hard to solve it; repeat.

This approach is familiar, comfortable, and has served them well in the past. The challenge arises when these uber-capable contributors are promoted to leadership roles where they direct cross-functional projects and are responsible for the work of others. Given their widened span of responsibilities, these professionals often stumble, experiencing a disconnect between their former success strategy and what their new charter requires.

What do you do when the way you have always done your job no longer works? How can you be successful when you're no longer measured by your ability to produce results on your own? A bumpy transition for many, it is possible to learn to thrive in this new context. It requires a willingness to reframe your focus and strategies for how you "win" on the job.

As an individual contributor, you can be laser-focused on the technical aspects of work; however, as a leader, you need to harness the efforts of others to do your job well. To accomplish this, you need to become aware of an *additional* layer of interaction beyond the work itself—how people are showing up. It requires learning to listen in a new way, beyond the words being spoken. Like in the movie *The Matrix*, there is a whole other plane of activity going on, and you need to tune into it.

The fastest way to tune in is to grow your capacity for noticing. For example, in a meeting notice if others are engaged, whether there seems to be alignment on the strategic direction being taken, and whether there are any apparent disagreements or disconnects not being sufficiently addressed. If you don't prioritize this level of awareness and interaction, you risk not being recognized as a truly impactful leader—at best, you will continue to be seen as an excellent "doer." You may find that this perception limits your upward mobility.

When you enter a meeting, your most important objective is to tune into the vibe of the people around you. Why? Because that is where the true action is happening. Here are some ways to practice those skills, stepping back from the details to pay attention to what is happening around you in any interaction:

- Prepare in advance so you already know your objective, constraints, and desired outcomes. This frees your attention to establish and maintain ongoing connections with others. If it feels hard to squeeze this prep into your already busy schedule, consider introducing the Morning Scan, which I will describe in a moment, into your routine.

- Avoid the temptation to focus only on the details of *your* agenda; rather, invite others to confirm their needs. Ask, "What do you want to get out of the meeting?" Probe what is important to them, what they are worried about, and, most importantly, how they will know their issues have been addressed. Repeat what you hear to make sure you have understood and incorporate those priorities into the discussion. Return periodically to the co-created agenda to make sure key points are addressed for all participants.

- If the items important to others are *not* part of the immediate agenda, quickly determine and communicate an appropriate forum for follow-up. Consider instituting a "parking lot" where you can write down these points in a visible fashion, perhaps on an actual or virtual whiteboard or in notes. This allows others to feel heard and to relax, knowing that the topics have been captured and will be addressed later.

- During the session, regularly look up to notice people's body language. Who is open? Who is closed? What are their facial expressions? Who seems to not be engaged? Adjust the way you interact to speak to their withdrawal, engagement, curiosity, or worry. Draw people out with open-ended questions and make space for them to answer.

Noticing energy and presence in others and modifying your approach to address those nuances can make all the difference between achieving the outcomes you need from any interaction or falling short.

Perform the Morning Scan

Sandra had been called out in several meetings for insufficient preparation, poor listening, and the inability to answer senior leadership's questions. Motivated to prevent this dynamic from recurring, she came to me for guidance.

Prior to her current role, Sandra had done a valiant job of staying on top of things. Now, directing the work of others and with leadership responsibility across multiple domains, she found herself reactive rather than proactive. She felt and acted distracted in meetings, multitasked when single-threaded attention was warranted, and canceled meeting attendance at the last-minute or arrived late. Left unchecked, these behaviors would have a negative impact on her reputation and advancement. Already these behaviors were undermining trust in her abilities among Sandra's leadership, peers, and direct reports.

For Sandra, increasing levels of responsibility and scope were layered on top of a pre-existing full workload. At the same time, the number of hours in the day did not increase, requiring the need to cover more ground in less time. The good news for Sandra—and for you if you suffer from similar circumstances—is that the remedy is straightforward and relatively easy to implement. It starts with the Morning Scan, a daily ritual that takes 30 to 60 minutes to execute. Yes, it adds a bit of time to your morning routine but is well worth the effort because it keeps your attention focused on where your efforts will be of highest value. Here's how to integrate it into each workday:

1. Start by scanning your key projects at a high level, noticing what short-term milestones need to be hit and what ongoing issues are most detrimental if not solved.

2. Next, review your daily and weekly calendar for commitments you've made and meetings to attend. Note where space exists—or doesn't exist—to get actual work done, collaboratively or heads-down.
3. Compile a shortlist of three to five items you will focus on today.

Next, wrangle your top priorities. For the balance of your allotted Morning Scan time, focus on your shortlisted items, making significant progress against completing them—or at least getting your hands around them. Map any remaining tasks to open windows in your calendar, finding ways to reclaim time to tackle these items if needed. To gain even more insight, consider performing the Weekly Scan. During that review, scan your upcoming week and determine where to make proactive changes to your schedule and communication strategy to accommodate anticipated priorities.

Daily and weekly scan habits can feel awkward and unnatural at first. But practicing these rituals enables you to lead from a place of intention rather than of reactivity. With time, the results you enjoy will promote a better allocation of resources, improved outcomes for the company and team, and ultimately a sense of career momentum.

Call on your future self

Laurie arrived for coaching filled with anxiety. A Chief Operations Officer with a strong track record in digital health leadership, she found herself at a career crossroads. Laurie worried what others would think if she went for the type of role that truly appealed to her now, which was neither in the C-suite nor in digital health. Conflicted, she hesitated to activate her robust network to obtain the role she desired, thinking she should go for the opposite. Her inner critic loomed large in her head, saying:

- People will be disappointed in me if I take my career in a new direction.
- The optics of the move won't look right on my resume or LinkedIn.
- I won't be able to come back from this if I make a mistake.
- No one else I know is making a move like this.
- People I care about have advised me against doing this.

These fears impeded material progress in her job search. In essence, Laurie was at war with herself, experiencing a push-me-pull-you energy that kept her deadlocked. To move forward, she needed to look beyond her fears to imagine the anticipated lived reality of each path under consideration so she could make an informed, whole-hearted decision. By viewing these possible futures with her non-negotiables in hand, she could guide herself to the other side of the dilemma, overcoming her strong resistance to picking a path.

With coaching, Laurie imagined both lives, envisioning herself a year or two out while considering what was most important to her. From that perspective, the path forward became clear. Laurie's next role would *not* be as a C-level executive but rather as one's right-hand. There, she could use her skills to make a difference, building her repertoire of accomplishments in scaling a company while minimizing her effort. Later, when she was ready, Laurie could parlay that experience into the C-suite or another direction of her choosing. Her chosen path felt congruent with her personal priorities, which included navigating a cross-country move for her family within the year, getting involved in politics, and providing steady support for her teenagers while her spouse led a fast-scaling startup. Although her chosen path still felt challenging, she now felt solid in her conviction to follow it, and able to make forward progress.

If you find yourself sitting at a professional crossroads like Laurie, where your inner guide is urging you to take an alternate path from the one you are on, know that you too can make a full-bodied, informed decision by tapping into your future self. From such a crossroads, you can consider at least two paths, including:

1. Staying on your current career path, taking the steps that feel logically next in line given your trajectory to date. By reaching for new challenges and/or the next rung on the ladder, you—and others—can see that you are continuing to advance and doing work commensurate with your experience and seniority.
2. Doing something different, getting quiet and listening to your inner guide calling for something off the beaten path. By reassuring yourself that it doesn't matter what others think, you can proceed in a different direction than what is expected.

Neither path is necessarily the right one! The trick is to figure out which is the right one for you, at least for now. You may visit similar crossroads at various times in your career; sometimes you may pick the first path, while other times you may pick the second. Either path can evoke uncomfortable feelings and involve challenges, even once you've decided in which direction to head.

If you decide to pursue path #1, it typically involves challenging yourself to change things up, perhaps by moving up to a position of larger scope and responsibility. As a result, you must gather your courage to clearly articulate your value commensurate with the scale of the opportunity you are walking into. On path #1 you have the best chance of addressing your heart's desire for something different by embedding some of your non-negotiables into your new chapter.

If you decide to take the less-traveled path, you need to continually ground yourself in what you truly want. This helps you maintain the courage to continue when you encounter resistance from others. You may have to explain and re-explain what you are planning to do and your rationale, as your course may veer from others' paths and/or their expectations of you. This requires staying centered on your North Star.

More and more I'm finding that mid-career professionals are opting for path #2 to make their life feel well-lived. Rather than wait for a post-fifty (or post-sixty) second career opportunity, they are choosing to follow a path of delight and meaning now. Know that if you choose to follow your internal compass and pursue path #2, there is ALWAYS a way to productively and positively message such a move. The most important ingredient is to be clear and have conviction.

If you find yourself at a similar crossroads, consider which direction makes sense for you now. Engage your mind as well as your heart and gut/intuition to tune into your personal energy. Then bring one of the paths you are considering into your mind, imagining you are either one, two, five, or ten years into the future looking back to today. With that lens, ponder these prompts:

- Here's what has been possible because of the decision to follow this path
  - ◊ For me:
  - ◊ For others I care about:
  - ◊ For the people I serve in my work:
- The thing I'm most proud of about having chosen this path is _____
- The experiences this path has afforded me include

  _____
- The drawbacks or challenges I've had to navigate because of choosing this path include _____
- What I would have liked to know when I made this decision to follow this path that I know now is _____
- What has made this path so fulfilling is _____

Now, imagine taking the other path, bringing it into your mind and repeating the above prompts. As you reflect, notice how your spirit feels and what path feels like the right one for you now. As needed, you can run small experiments and hold conversations with others to further inform your decision. However, if you are like Laurie, you have done a lot of listening to voices outside yourself already; tuning into your inner guide through your future self can help you reach a wholehearted decision.

Regardless of the path you decide to select now, know that you will have future opportunities to make either a similar choice or head in a new direction.

PAY ATTENTION ON MULTIPLE LEVELS

Active listening involves taking in data on multiple levels, including body language and the energy behind the message, allowing us to grasp a lot more information than simply the words being exchanged. With these additional details, we can take care of our own needs while also addressing those of others. This enables us to do our finest work, producing better outcomes with less effort and solving multi-dimensional problems at their root.

7. BROADEN YOUR BASE OF SUPPORT

From Alone and Isolated to Connected and Amplified

THE TRAP: TRYING TO DO IT ALL YOURSELF

Vanessa couldn't believe it. Yet another one of her colleagues had landed a new job! The company was in the process of being acquired, and people were abandoning ship right and left. The acquiring company's leaders were steamrolling over everything. This included the culture and projects that Vanessa and her colleagues had so carefully constructed. The result? They felt trampled upon.

Vanessa had seen the writing on the wall long before the acquisition had been announced and had been looking for a new job for months. She could not count how many applications she had submitted! As a result, this latest defection especially stung. Her direct report had found a new job quickly and was leaving to take what Vanessa considered to be her dream role. Ouch.

Vanessa felt lonely and bleary-eyed sitting at her

computer late at night, scrolling through jobs and sending applications into the void. How did her colleague land such a great new job so quickly? The next day Vanessa asked how she landed the new position. "Connections," the person responded. "I networked my way in." Vanessa let out a deep sigh. It all came back to networking, her least favorite activity.

Vanessa fell prey to the sixth trap I see executives fall into: operating from a narrow base of support. In her job search, Vanessa was focused one-dimensionally, not on her network but on submitting one job application after another. Meanwhile, her co-worker drew on a vibrant network of friends, colleagues, and business associates to help make introductions, advocate for her, and uncover opportunities, ultimately to secure an appealing new role.

Do you feel like you are repeatedly getting passed over for—or not even made aware of—new opportunities in the job market or in your company? If yes, you too may be suffering from a narrow base of support. To fix this you will need to prioritize activating, broadening, and diversifying your network. Only by harnessing the power of relation-ships to amplify your efforts can you gain access to the inside track for opportunities you want.

OVERCOME YOUR RESISTANCE TO ASKING FOR HELP

While her colleague drew on a vibrant set of connections to obtain her new position, Vanessa's network languished. Her colleague had invested in growing and maintaining professional relationships; Vanessa had not. The results spoke for themselves. Her co-worker's contacts helped surface a job that met her requirements and then advocated for her as a good fit. In contrast, Vanessa had no such team working for her.

Many professionals underinvest in nurturing a strong, active set of business relationships. If you don't like to talk about yourself, were brought up to be humble, are an introvert, don't want to look weak, don't want to bother people, don't know how to do it, or just can't be bothered, you may resist reaching out to others because doing so increases your sense of vulnerability.

Sure, it can feel uncomfortable to ask for help, and it takes time we often don't have. The effort requires us to solidify weak ties with people we don't know well and in some cases to invent reasons to interact with them. On the job we are trained to limit our exposure, hide our soft underbelly, and appear strong. Asking for help seemingly flies in the face of that logic.

However, being professionally vulnerable can lead to dialogue that benefits both you AND others. You gain access to needed information and opportunities; others gain the satisfaction of sharing their experience and being of assistance to you. Now more than ever people long to make a difference. It feels good to help someone else and invites reciprocity in the future. The person helping may even benefit personally, earning a referral bonus, being seen as a hero for sourcing the right candidate, or solving a problem after discussing their challenges with you.

The actual *practice* of networking is quite simple, a set of repeatable steps. What makes it challenging is the *attitude* we bring to it. We don't want to bother anyone, so rather than ask for a personal introduction, we simply send a resume in response to a company's job posting. We don't know what to talk about, so we avoid requesting regular one-on-ones with our peers to develop stronger relationships. We want to avoid rejection, so when a recruiter offers to distribute our resume to their network, we procrastinate about sending them the document.

When networking one-on-one, conversations may seem awkward and unfocused at first. With honesty, integrity, and collaboration, these touchpoints can mature into longstanding, mutually beneficial relationships. Discussing individual challenges and offering feedback, ideas, and support to resolve those obstacles is often the focus of these conversations.

Peter, a global CIO, calls these touchpoints "Get Smart Sessions." In each meeting he brings his colleague up to speed on what his team is working on and solicits an update about his peer's progress against key initiatives. Together, they then strategize how he and his colleague can best be of service to one another. His peer continues the quarterly meetings because they produce valuable takeaways.

My colleague Meredith recommends that if networking feels difficult to you, start with your inner circle. Seek out those you know best and solidify those bonds first. By holding conversations with relatively low-stakes folks, you can practice asking open-ended questions with people who care about you and know how good you are. You can request introductions to others in positions of influence to expand your network. One executive found herself referred for several job opportunities and securing her target role within two months by using this technique!

Underinvesting in networking is a key reason many people remain stuck in situations they don't want. Transformational change happens through connections and relationships, period. You simply cannot gain access to the quality information and opportunities you need any other way.

TAKE ADVANTAGE OF EXISTING POWER STRUCTURES

Scott felt like he was living a bad dream. Having spent the last eight years heads-down leading a global architecture team, he had hoped his good work would speak for itself. However, in the latest performance cycle, Scott learned he was being passed over for promotion again. He watched enviously as two of his peers advanced to the next level. Why them and not him? He felt both disappointed and annoyed.

Reflecting, Scott noticed something about his two colleagues: they had regular facetime one-on-one with their boss. In contrast, his time with their boss was infrequent and focused on tactical issues. In fact, Scott's one-on-ones were often canceled. He didn't prioritize rescheduling them because he didn't see much value in them. He wondered what his colleagues talked about in their sessions with the boss.

Thinking further, Scott noticed that his colleagues regularly reported their latest findings from cross-aisle peers in team meetings. They seemed in the know about what was happening in other areas, while Scott didn't enjoy that same visibility. When did they have time to connect? An introvert, Scott sensed he *should* be networking more but was unsure how to go about it, and the idea made him uncomfortable. He didn't want to impose on others and wasn't sure what to talk about should he successfully snag a spot on his colleagues' calendars.

These realizations served as a wake-up call. Scott could see that by not accessing leadership and building collaborative relationships, he missed small opportunities every week. Over time, these issues added up to a significant disparity between how he was viewed as a leader and how his peers were.

WEAVE A STRONG WEB

When a spider weaves its web, the process is methodical, takes effort, and produces an elegant, resilient mesh. The web is designed to flexibly move in the breeze while staying intact, catching opportunities—in the form of flies or other insects—as they come along. Networking is similar: weave a strong web to reach opportunities beyond your personal grasp.

With coaching, Scott discovered that although he enjoyed the technical aspects of his job, he longed to make a larger impact. Now that he could see the dynamics at play, he felt motivated to build a strong web of his own. Over the next six months, Scott developed a strategic agenda to build his influence. He held regular one-on-ones with his boss to discuss strategic issues. He prioritized his time more effectively, reserving space and energy for higher leverage activities like networking. Scott created regular touchpoints with his internal stakeholders, partnering to exchange information and collaborate on thorny challenges.

Scott helped his team, supervisor, and colleagues benefit

from the intel he gathered about trends in the larger organization. These insights allowed them to better serve their stakeholders. In fact, one initiative garnered the company an industry award! It was an exciting moment that further solidified for Scott the importance of a strong web.

His next performance review was a completely different conversation than the previous one. Scott's efforts to develop himself and expand his impact impressed his superiors, resulting in an increased span of responsibility and a promotion.

PRACTICES AND TACTICS

Networking may sound tough, but a few key best practices make it an easy, repeatable process that produces dividends. Invest in some of these approaches to expand your reach, whether looking to land your next role or increase influence where you are. Your objective here is an increased sense of *stability*—feeling the support of your strong web, with people and processes to access to stay connected, informed, and to minimize your sense of vulnerability. These practices and tactics partner well with the free bonus tools you can access at **www.yourfinestwork.com** to help you improve your sense of stability.

Set up the scaffolding you need

You exponentially increase your chance of success with career transformation by building the structure and support you need around you. This includes making a realistic plan for what the effort will take, enrolling the guidance you need, letting people who care about you know so they can be supportive, and establishing foolproof ways to stay accountable and on track.

Ask yourself:

- What does this process require of me on a weekly/ regular basis to be successful? How much time do I need to reserve, and where in my calendar will I fit that time in?
- What am I willing to start doing to have the best chance of success?
- What am I willing to stop doing?
- What support do I need?
- What methods work best for me to successfully navigate changes that require persistence and courage?
- What is my game plan if things get off track for me with this project?

With these answers in hand, you can start designing your career transformation project with the infrastructure you need to be successful. If you are like me and do better keeping commitments to others than to yourself, consider hiring an executive coach or enrolling in a group to provide accountability. Just as when you pay a personal trainer or attend a regular exercise class to help you exercise, having an accountability buddy or support team can make it easier to keep the commitment to yourself. A coaching relation-ship or group program can also provide a roadmap to follow to make the changes you crave, like those outlined in this book, so you don't have to think so much about *how* you will make the change and instead focus on *what* you want to change.

With the decision made to make a career change and a six-month runway before proactively leaving my job, I hired a career counselor to help me identify and evaluate options for my next line of work. As you may recall, I was living with the very real possibility that I might never have children, so everything was on the table: what kind of life and, by extension, what kind of career did I want to have? My weekly meetings with my career counselor, Sepha, felt like sacred time; I prioritized them over everything else.

Sepha guided me to clarify my values, identify the types of job duties I enjoyed, and try on different career directions. Through this process I identified two possible paths for my next career. With research and experimentation, I ultimately boiled it down to one. Her thoughtful process connected me to my internal guide and inspired me to push through obstacles in my path.

The speed at which you can move and the amount of ground you can cover are directly proportional to the amount of time, energy, and focused attention you are willing to devote. If your current schedule limits you to an hour or two per week focused on implementing the strategies in this book, your transformation may occur at a slower pace. If you are extremely motivated to change your situation as soon as possible, a weekly allotment of time may require five to ten hours or more for these same activities. The good news is that any time you can carve out on a regular basis is valuable.

An incremental approach can be powerful, with a few

hours per week devoted to working on what is important to you. Like exercising regularly or eating whole, unprocessed foods, cultivating more of what you want for your professional life is a career-long practice providing long-term benefits. Just as a savings account grows your wealth through regular deposits, your ongoing investment in growing your career will pay dividends throughout your life.

Foster strong relationships throughout the organization

It's easy to avoid prioritizing proactive relationship building, especially if you are an introvert or feel overworked already. However, prioritizing relationship building makes all the difference when the inevitable happens: changes in the leadership around you.

Nancy and Daniel had worked well together in a prior company, so he hired her again to lead a new organization to similar success. Over the year they worked side by side at the new company, Nancy had continued to build her relationship with Daniel, driving the strategic work of the business. Since she considered them attached at the hip, it took her completely by surprise when he abruptly announced he was leaving. Nancy felt shocked, angry, disappointed, fearful, and vulnerable, finding herself suddenly without an advocate in leadership to vouch for her value.

Daniel left with minimal fanfare. He was preoccupied with his new role and unconcerned with making the transition a smooth one for Nancy. She had put her trust in him and felt let down. It was as if she were rowing in a heavy river current without a paddle, struggling to gain her bearings without capsizing.

When Nancy arrived for coaching, she was in the throes of being tossed about by this change. Our first step was to help her see that although she had not caused this event, she was responsible for the impact it had on her. To her credit, Nancy grasped this immediately. Choosing not to play the victim, she took the opportunity to learn from the situation and move forward productively. She planned to stay on in the company and wanted to thrive there, so she needed to come to terms with the change and rebound from its negative impacts. This involved her spending time and effort in two areas: 1) healing her hurt feelings; and 2) building new relationships with a wide array of stakeholders.

When a situation like this occurs, emotions naturally run high. Whether the feelings are anger, frustration, disappointment, embarrassment, shame, betrayal, fear, or something else, they don't just dissipate on their own. Like a tea kettle whistling when the water boils, it's necessary to release the pressure such emotions create. Only then can a person put down resentment or residual feelings and move on effectively. It is not only wise but necessary to create a means to release and process strong feelings.

In coaching, healing becomes part of the conversation. We need to clear the energetic hurdle so the person can constructively move on. In Nancy's case, she did a few things:

- wrote a letter to her departing boss—that she didn't send—letting him know exactly what she thought about what he had done
- crafted a list of her non-negotiables for the type of

relationship she wanted to develop with her new boss going forward

- started a woodworking project at home that had her hammering nails into wood, a satisfying way to release stress
- upped her regular exercise routine to release the stress that her hurt feelings had engendered

The letter writing is a technique from master coach Maria Nemeth, founder of the Academy of Coaching Excellence and the author of *Mastering Life's Energies: Simple Steps to a Luminous Life at Work and Play,* New World Library; 1st edition (February 23, 2007). It involves reflecting on what you really want to say to someone and would communicate, unfiltered, if there were no ramifications.

After writing the letter out by hand, you rip it up, shred, or burn it, disposing of the debris outside your office or living space. Then you ritualistically wash your hands and arms with soap for twenty seconds or longer to remove the negative energy you've been dealing with. Nancy found the letter writing to be particularly helpful. She repeated the exercise a second time to reduce the impact her thoughts about her boss' actions had on her.

Nancy next turned her attention to building a cross-functional array of stakeholder relationships to strengthen and expand her professional footing. To avoid feeling orphaned again, she compiled a list of senior leaders she respected, would be delighted to get to know better, and who worked in areas where she felt she could add value.

Nancy organized her list into tiers to segment her efforts.

Those in her Tier A cohort received more of her attention than Tier B. Over time, she implemented networking strategies that brought her into regular contact with these leaders. In these interactions both parties benefitted, which made her feel more secure. When one departed, she filled the slot with another leader to strengthen bonds up and across the company. With her new manager and skip-level leader, she focused on developing deep ties with a sense of detachment, realizing that these relationships were not the only ones to nurture.

As she made networking a habit, Nancy was surprised to find her job satisfaction increase. She heightened her influence by increasing her face time with senior leaders. Her networking efforts sat on top of relationships she had always prioritized—those with her direct reports and subordinates. However, even those connections improved. To grow strong relationships with senior colleagues, she had to become efficient with her time, and so she empowered her team more.

To build a strong web of your own in your current organization, consider assessing how you are doing within three lanes of relationship building: across, up, and down the company. Compile a list of people you would benefit from interacting with beyond typical meetings, and consider organizing the list into tiers, identifying different levels of interaction and effort commensurate with each one. Choose a cross section of folks you admire and respect as well as those who are more challenging for you. If you feel that a relationship is contentious or subpar, it can be worth investing in to move beyond those differences and forge a mutually beneficial working relationship. If you are between roles, consider a similar strategy, developing a set of relationships with former peers, superiors, and subordinates.

These ongoing feedback loops strengthen your personal web; as a result, others will keep their eyes and ears open for your priorities and bring opportunities to your attention. Once you establish your relationship-building routines, you may be pleasantly surprised, as Nancy was, with how they can run like clockwork. You can evolve your techniques over time to get the most out of the relationships with the least effort, producing valuable outcomes for all.

Try three things, three ways, three times

When you put yourself out there to connect with other leaders, it takes courage. It can feel discouraging when you don't receive a positive response or, worse yet, no response at all. It can be hard to keep going when this happens, but it is important to persevere, up to a point.

Gate your effort with any one contact, giving it your full attention up until a certain point, and then if you don't get the response you are looking for, move on. In other words, try three things, three ways, three times.

Let's say that your old boss introduces you to a leader you had wanted to meet. You hold an informational interview with that person. As part of the discussion, the leader promises to introduce you to a colleague hiring for your desired role. You leave the meeting agreeing he will do that.

And then he doesn't. After the meeting, you send a thank you note, showing gratitude for his time and anticipating the introduction. A few days go by, and you receive neither a response nor an introduction. You ping him via email to check in and remind him of his commitment. You include a short blurb he can attach to the introduction to make it as easy as possible.

A few days more go by, and you hear nothing. You give it one more try by leaving him a voicemail. After a few more days and no response, it's time to move on. Either go directly to the contact to introduce yourself, or find another avenue to make the connection. If the original person eventually reaches out to make good on the promise to introduce you, great; however, you are not waiting for it to happen. With internal networking, a similar approach can apply.

Expending a fixed amount of energy allows your brain to relax, knowing that the effort spent beyond your comfort zone will be limited. You may find that on the third ping, the person *finally* responds, apologizing for not having gotten back to you before. Don't throw in the towel too early, but avoid pushing past a reasonable point. You can adjust your approach and the number of attempts to work for you.

AMPLIFY YOUR EFFORTS BY HARNESSING THE POWER OF OTHERS

Networking is a practice you can learn, AND you can't afford NOT to do it. Countless professionals who once avoided networking report that once they get into the practice of it, it's surprisingly fruitful. Reconnecting with old colleagues, catching up on what they have been up to and where they are headed, can rekindle a friendship. These touchpoints can facilitate a warm introduction to someone who ends up

being a significant connection for you. People secure jobs
and other opportunities, such as speaking engagements,
from conversations with their neighbor's nephew or their
prior boss' sister. You never know where conversations
may lead and where the gold may be!

8. SHARPEN YOUR PROFESSIONAL NARRATIVE

From Missing the Mark to Hitting Your Target

THE TRAP: FAILING TO CRAFT A COMPELLING CAREER STORY

Padma, a senior director in a technology company, came to coaching unsure how to reach her career goals. She had been applying for new opportunities over the past six months but had achieved little traction. She felt frustrated because although she had updated her resume and LinkedIn profile, she was neither receiving responses to her job applications nor progressing past the first round of interviews for inbound opportunities.

A recruiter friend offered to review her materials, concluding that she was not presenting her candidacy in a way that spoke to the needs of the roles and employers she was targeting. As a result, the recruiter deduced, she was being passed over in favor of other candidates whose materials did resonate. A feeling of futility brought her to coaching.

When Padma first practiced her interview answers with me, she sounded like she was reading off a cue card. In response to the prompt, "Tell me about yourself," she regurgitated a list of the jobs she had held. Although informative, her answer wasn't particularly memorable. Padma's resume, LinkedIn profile, and interview answers outlined where she had been in her career but not where she was headed. I didn't feel anything when she shared them with me and found myself stifling a yawn.

Padma had fallen prey to the seventh trap I see with leaders I coach: failing to tell a compelling story about her career. Do you feel like you are repeatedly getting passed over for, or not even made aware of, new opportunities in the job market or in your company? If yes, you too may be suffering from underinvesting in this powerful career asset. To fix this you will need to spend some concentrated effort sharpening your professional narrative to make it truly sing for your current and future employers to consider you for new opportunities.

BLEND WHERE YOU'VE BEEN WITH WHERE YOU'RE HEADED

A key flaw in most professional narratives I see is that they focus on a person's past instead of their future. It may sound counterintuitive to consider this a flaw—aren't a resume, LinkedIn profile, elevator pitch, and set of interview answers supposed to describe what you've done?

Yes and no.

Yes, you need to describe what you've done and

accomplished, but through the lens of what you want to do next. In other words, you must highlight the past work you have enjoyed and de-emphasize the job duties and accomplishments that have drained you and you don't care to do again. The purpose of your compelling story is to convey a clear picture of what you want to do in the future, backed up by concrete evidence of how you have done that same or similar thing in the past.

The overwhelming majority of the resumes and LinkedIn profiles I review— and I've reviewed thousands of them— spend either no or minimal space and language up front translating for the reader who the person is, including how their experience fits what the target employer is looking for. Instead, they include a rundown of the companies, roles, dates, and duties that make up the person's employment history. Similarly, the standard interview question, "Tell me about yourself" is often answered with a run-through of one's employment history, as Padma did. Both approaches can get you knocked out of contention for an opportunity you want, and fast.

Your compelling story is about so much more than the jobs you have held; rather, it is the dynamic account you share with yourself and others about who you are, what you are on this planet to do, and the impact you make. It is authentic, revealing your personality and what is important to you. It is relevant, applying your experience to how your target audience frames their requirements, so they can recognize their need for you. It is relatable, presented in a way that is both interesting and easily understood. Finally, it is consistent, shared across platforms, presenting a cohesive picture to the world.

A tight synopsis that can be scaled up or down to apply to a variety of situations, your compelling story is both an account of what you enjoy doing and what others value in you. Though it can be easily tweaked to fit any situation, when crafted intentionally, its underlying message remains consistent. You may dress it up slightly to add keywords for a particular role, but fundamentally it is a solid template for all positions you apply for. Your compelling story can be used to convey your style, experience, and impact in a variety of situations, including:

- applying for jobs
- interviewing for a new role
- going for a promotion or taking on additional responsibility
- seeking a board role
- being introduced for a speaking engagement
- securing speaking engagements
- networking with leaders in positions of influence
- fostering strategic relationships
- publishing articles or a book

The content is compiled by blending the following: 1) who you are, what lights you up, and how you like to add value, 2) what your target audience wants and needs from the role, 3) your professional experience and accomplishments that support both #1 and #2.

These three ingredients, together, reveal a powerful narrative, informing both your external dialogue in terms of how you talk with others and your internal dialogue in terms of how you talk to yourself. Being seen as a credible candidate for an opportunity comes from knowing what you stand for while sharing your experience in a way that addresses what your target—and/or current—employer wants and needs from you.

INSPIRE CONFIDENCE IN YOUR AUDIENCE

When networking for a new job or an advancement opportunity in your existing organization, your goal is to inspire confidence in others. In my experience, inspiring confidence results from embodying four qualities which work together to make you memorable and promote you through the process.

1. **Enthusiasm:** your energy and positivity for the role on offer, the arena the company plays in, and the organization's impact on its stakeholders.
2. **Competence:** your demonstrated ability to perform the duties inherent in the role.
3. **Relevance:** your experience in the field and the degree to which you understand and embody the values and culture of the organization.
4. **Presence:** how grounded, well-spoken, poised, and confident you are, attuned to what is happening real-time in the interview and adapting to meet the moment.

Enthusiasm and presence are related to your *being*—who you are and how you show up. Competence and relevance stem from your *doing*—what you've accomplished, what you are capable of, and what you will do in the future. You make a positive impression when your being AND doing match the expectations held by those making the decision about the role or advancement opportunity.

Enthusiasm naturally emerges when you are genuinely interested. Without it, you neither progress to the next round of interviews nor sustain the engagement of a prospective partner. Enthusiasm is obvious in your countenance—your eyes and smile in particular—and is often accompanied by a sense of lightness, positivity, and flow. In a job search, asking intentional, well-researched, and open-ended questions displays your enthusiasm for the mission of the organization and charter of the role. On the job, showing interest in understanding your colleagues and helping them succeed shows your enthusiasm too.

Competence derives from your prior experience doing similar work. In job interviews and advancement conversations, your competence is revealed by sharing succinct, compelling examples of your accomplishments, a clear understanding of the business challenges inherent in the role, and concrete strategies for how to solve problems.

Relevance means you are a cultural and social fit. In a job search, your awareness, articulation, and relish for the role's challenges and opportunities help you embody the intangible qualities the company values. Use your targeted career story, examples of past work, and company research to showcase your candidacy in the most relevant light.

When networking internally, relevance looks like being sensitive to what is going on in the larger ecosystem of the company and offering tools and strategies to help your colleagues be successful.

Presence emerges from both grounding and gravitas. Being prepared helps you slow down. Guided meditations, breathing exercises, and other mindfulness practices quiet your inner critic and enable you to focus on your message and rapport building. Confident, open body language communicates credibility and deep listening, elevating the quality of the conversation.

These four qualities are powerful levers you can push on when you are not gaining adequate traction in your networking, whether in a job search or within your current organization. Where are you underinvesting? Where have you relied too much on one quality and not enough on another? Consider experiments to run to right-size the four qualities to increase your ability to inspire confidence in others.

PRACTICES AND TACTICS

With your compelling story honed and practiced, you naturally upgrade the quality of your networking. The synergy of being able to articulate clearly what you want, stand for, and bring to the table lends you an air of assuredness and distinction. Rather than appear needy or desperate, you appear content and discerning. This makes you more appealing as a candidate, with examples you can easily share underlining your value to current and future employers. Your overall goal here is a sense of *self-confidence*. When you know what to say and how to say it, you can relax more and show up as your most powerful. The assessment and action-planning tools available at **www.yourfinestwork.com** can also help.

Reverse engineer what your target market needs

Imagine a hiring manager or recruiter reviewing your qualifications against what they are looking for and checking off their requirements as they go. "Yes, they've done this, and this, and this. It looks like they have what we need! Let's bring them in for an interview." This is the reaction you are going for with your compelling story.

To get there you must marry what you enjoy and the value you create with what your target employer is looking for. The good news is that there is a straightforward way to do this: studying, organizing, and employing content from the job description they have provided. You are not copying the job description; rather, you are using it to help you understand what they are prioritizing and how to bring those elements out of your experience and what you plan to do next, career-wise. It works well to blend two or three job descriptions that appeal to you together to confirm what the roles that appeal to you require in terms of core competencies, functional expertise, and experience.

Here's how to do it:

1. Pull out one of your target job listings. Copy the content into a new document and save the file.

2. Go through the content with a virtual highlighter, marking the phrases and keywords that the employer is asking for, placing special focus on items that you have some experience with and enjoy.

3. Delete everything that is not highlighted.

4. Sort the job duties and qualifications into themes. Come up with a name for each theme, shooting for three to five themes total. For example, if several bullet points have to do with "Facilitating cross-functional collaboration," then group those together under that header. Continue until you have sorted and categorized all the items you highlighted into themes.

5. Put the themes in the order that makes sense to you.

6. Copy another target job description into this document and repeat the steps above, blending the content from the new job description with the old one.

7. If you have a third target job description, repeat the process.

With two or three target job descriptions incorporated, you'll identify 90 percent or more of the requirements you need to showcase in your compelling story to make a strong case for yourself as a candidate for these roles.

Now that you have a good idea of what your target employers are looking for in terms of skills and competencies, you can frame your experience and what you enjoy doing against these requirements, using similar language to what they are asking for so they recognize their need for you. This may include adding a section up front to charac-terize yourself and your experience, as well as peppering in the ideas and language you culled from your analysis of the job descriptions into your accomplishments.

Refine your elevator pitch and career headline

To grab your audience's attention and entice them to want to learn more, you need an easy-to-digest, appealing blurb that rolls off your tongue while capturing your professional impact, breadth of experience, and key traits. Your elevator pitch serves double duty: it's both the thing you say in net-working situations and the wording you display on the top of your resume or LinkedIn profile. Your career headline imparts what you stand for and are in this world to do, summarized in a single phrase.

Most leaders I coach are intimidated by the prospect of coming up with an elevator pitch and career headline. However, the process to draft them is actually quite easy: just follow the prompts. To make it even less intimidat-ing, consider approaching the process in two phases, first focusing on making sure the ideas are the ones you want to share, and then later polishing the language to make what you have drafted sound great. This sequencing removes the paralyzing need to make each sentence production-ready from the get-go. Rather, like an artist, you let the picture emerge gradually, compiling the ideas and then stepping back with a critical eye to refine them into a tight narrative that feels both authentic and impressive.

To refine your elevator pitch and career headline, consider noodling one or both of the following reflection exercises.

Reflection A

Fill in the following prompts:

1. Who you are:
2. What you do:
3. How you do it:
4. Why you do it:
5. Who you do it for:
6. Now, consolidate the various answers above into 1–2 sentences. This is your first rough draft.

Reflection B

Fill in the following prompts:

1. The problem you solve:
2. Why it matters to solve this problem:
3. How you solve it:
4. Who you solve it for:
5. The impact/benefit that your solving the problem has:
6. Now, consolidate the various answers above into 1–2 sentences. This is your second rough draft.

Next:

1. Review your two rough drafts, consolidating your content into one. Play with your new draft until you find a version you like best, condensing it down to a sentence or two. Imagine sharing it with someone else; speak it out loud and see how it rolls off your tongue. This is your working elevator pitch.
2. Identify a story that illustrates you solving a problem. Frame a sentence you can share, as

appropriate, after your elevator pitch, to exemplify your good work. Go through the prompts above to make sure you have covered all the bases with your story.

3. Stand back and see what overarching, simple theme surfaces as the essence of what you do and how you do it. You can even lift portions of your elevator pitch language verbatim. This is your draft career headline.

With these drafts in hand reflect on what you like about them and what needs further refinement. Consider where you can post both in a place you will see them each day to keep them top of mind, such as attached to your bathroom mirror, in your closet, or by your bedside. Also, consider which two or three people you can share the drafts with over the next week to solicit some feedback.

The goal here is not to come up with the perfect blurb for your elevator pitch and career headline; rather, it is to get solid, good enough versions of each compiled so you can road test and continue to refine them. We are looking to remove the obstacle of not having a working elevator pitch and career headline so you can get on with your networking toward your finest work.

Shape your accomplishments

You master your compelling story when your accomplishments blend three ingredients:

1. what you have done in the past
2. what your target employer is asking for
3. what you want / your non-negotiables

It may sound daunting to combine these three pieces of data into cohesive achievements, but it is possible using PAR statements:

- P is for Problem
- A is for Action
- R is for Results

Note: PAR is like the STAR method, but I find it simpler to use. The process is completed in two parts.

Part 1: Journal about your favorite projects

1. **For each role you have held, make a list of up to three projects that felt especially satisfying to you.** Come up with a name to refer to each project. If you don't relate to the concept of single projects, think in terms of channels of work, meaning types of activities you have completed in each role. For example, you might have enjoyed processing insurance claims or preparing newsletters. What is most important is that it be work that you enjoy some or all aspects of. It is NOT important that it be the most important or successful part of your role; in fact, I once coached an attorney whose favorite project was a case that his firm lost! You may find that the farther back you go, the fewer projects you remember. Just go back as far as you can, with your primary focus on the past ten to fifteen years of your experience.

2. ***Starting with the most recent role, pick the first project.*** Write a few sentences describing the problem you were tasked by answering the following questions:
   a. What was the problem?
   b. What was not working, and what were you tasked to do about it?
   c. What was at risk for you, for the organization, and for others, if the problem remained unsolved?

Label this section, "Problem."

3. ***Now, label the next section, "Action."*** Document the actions you took or directed others to take to solve the problem. Don't worry about putting the steps in any order; rather, just record what comes up:
   a. What did you orchestrate, handle, plan, or implement?
   b. Who did you work with, wrangling their efforts to help solve the problem?
   c. What types of resources were involved?
   d. How long did it take?

Write as much as occurs to you here about what you did, or led others to do, under your direction.

4. ***Finally, write the results of your efforts in a section labeled "Results."***
   a. Was the problem solved, and if yes, how did you know?
   b. If money was saved, how much?

    c. If attrition was reduced, by what amount?

    d. If business was won, how much?

    e. How long did it take to solve?

    f. How many customers were impacted?

    g. How large was the team you managed to get the job done?

There is always a way to quantify the end results for a project, even if it is not immediately obvious. For example, one HR compliance leader reduced four one-thousand-page documents into one two-hundred-and-fifty-page document. You are looking to show the scale of the impact created by you solving the problem. Turn off your internal editor and just write what comes to you. If you need to look up the percentage of revenue increase resulting from the project, you can come back to it later. Don't get distracted by those details while journaling.

5. ***Repeat the above steps*** for each project for the current or most recent role you have held, then proceed through your prior roles, journaling answers to the same questions. If you can, limit the effort for each project to no more than five to ten minutes; this is not meant to be a taxing exercise, rather, a top-of-mind reflection. Once the journaling is done, step back for a bit and take a break.

Part 2: Draft your accomplishments

Next, string each of these projects' PAR content into draft accomplishment statements:

1. Make a copy of the journaled content for the first project for your current/most recent role, copying it right below the original content.
2. Taking a virtual highlighter, review the Problem, Action, and Results content, highlighting the words and phrases that capture the essence of the problem, the actions you took, and the results of your efforts.
3. Next, delete everything else (from that copied version, keeping the original version intact in case you need to refer back to it), so that you end up with a list of highlighted words and phrases. Dispense with the Problem, Action, and Results headers too.
4. Now draft an accomplishment, either one or two sentences in length, that summarizes the content you highlighted, using those very words you highlighted. Don't worry about making the phrasing sound polished; for now your focus is simply on stringing together the ideas into cohesive sentences. Make sure to include the impact your actions produced. Note: you will end up with a sentence or two that feels long and clunky; leave it be for now as you will refine and shorten it later.
5. Move on to the next project, repeating the steps outlined above, until you have gone through all the projects for all the roles.

6. When you are finished, copy draft accomplishment onto the front page of your document, listing them in reverse chronological order by role. Voila! You have the first version of your accomplishments ready for editing.

Engaging with what you have enjoyed across your various roles can instill a sense of continuity and career trajectory. When you see your accomplishments in this light, you realize the challenges you have faced and overcome have made you who you are today, uniquely qualified for what is next. Thinking about my own career, I learned more from working for a startup that failed than from any other stage of my professional life, except for running my own business. I find that often the experiences that most negatively impact us—representing what we don't want to replicate in future career steps—allows us to recognize what we truly want so we can evolve ever closer to our finest work going forward.

STELLAR STORYTELLING UNLOCKS EXCITING CAREER OPPORTUNITIES

With career coaching, Padma overhauled her internal and external professional narrative. She first compiled her non-negotiables to gain clarity about what she wanted. Next, she collected three target job descriptions, including the role one level above her current job, as well as two others that intrigued her outside the company. She reverse-engineered those listings to distill what her current and target employers were asking for so she could use their terminology to explain who she is, what she does, and the value she creates.

Next, she took an editing eye to her current narrative, identifying the facets of current and prior jobs that she most enjoyed. She drafted an updated elevator pitch and career headline, combining the language from the job descriptions with details about what was unique about her and how her experience provided proof of her ability to be successful in her target roles. Plus, she drafted new accomplishments outlining her favorite work projects to date, employing the PAR statements journaling exercise to flesh out the various aspects of her work and then editing down these experiences to their essence.

Your compelling story clearly and succinctly demonstrates how your experience makes you well suited for what's next. It serves as a gateway to the next phase of your career—and to your finest work. Once you clarify your targeted path, whether it be a new job, a new career, a new assignment, or a promotion, you naturally start to notice opportunities to make a case for having what you want. With a tight, impactful story to tell about your career, you can more easily take advantage of these openings.

Being fully seen for who you are, what you've accomplished, and your unique talents is validating. Do not underestimate the influence your compelling story can have on your self-confidence and, ultimately, your career success.

9. YOUR FORMULA FOR SUCCESS

Your finest work is achieved when you experience your own definition of fulfillment, impact, and success. Rather than a destination, it is a journey, a day-to-day experience, and a state of being.

The seven strategies laid out in the previous chapters work in concert to bring online the finest version of your career you've ever experienced. A sense of true livelihood—or as I call it, "Livelyhood"—comes from the interplay these seven strategies have on each other. The key to accessing your finest work is to attend to the seven strategies simultaneously, in an ongoing fashion. When you do, the rest takes care of itself. You achieve almost immediate gains once you start incorporating practices and tactics associated with the seven strategies, and you will enjoy increasing dividends over time as you remain devoted to them.

A NEW PLAYBOOK FOR TURBULENT TIMES

Cultivating your finest work requires attention to how the world is changing, both your inner world and the one around you. It is a combination of gaining clarity about what you want while also paying attention to and responding to what others need. And then taking action, one step at a time.

To have the career you long for, you must be willing to become intentional, take responsibility for yourself and your choices, and move from a place of being a passenger of your experience to being the architect of it. While the effort is significant, the payoff is tremendous. You gain clarity about your purpose, excitement to begin each day, confidence in your value and impact, and support from a wide-reaching, vibrant network. All of this can help you access and do your finest work, increasing your earning potential with ongoing growth and learning opportunities.

The only wrong move is to be unwilling to act on your own behalf and let others define your career trajectory. You are not too old to make a change, and it's possible to refine your existing role or retool yourself for a new arena. Even if you feel that you have stayed too long in your current position or pigeonholed yourself by only focusing on one set of skills, that doesn't mean change is out of reach.

Many of the leaders I coach are at a point where their professional journey is simply not progressing. Once they dig under the surface, it's surprising how often it is not the job itself that they are struggling with but rather their perspective that is the problem. By prioritizing the seven strategies, they reclaim energy for their career and steer it in the direction of their choosing, navigating skillfully.

REPAIR LEAKS IN THE SYSTEM

Some of the strategies and tactics outlined in this book may come more naturally to you, while others require more of your focus and attention to fully embody.

When you are not satisfied professionally and find your career does not meet your expectations, you are likely falling prey to one or more of the seven traps. Your feelings can be helpful in diagnosing where best to focus your attention to shift the situation by applying the appropriate strategies and tactics.

For example, when you feel like your career is happening to you, focus on *becoming your career's intentional architect.* This puts you on the path to self-determination by instilling a sense of control. Tactics and practices to try include making time to stare out the window, inviting yourself to the party, and deciding to make yourself and your needs a priority.

When you are feeling scattered and reactive, stop and spend some time gaining clarity on what you want and *defining your North Star.* Doing so results in a sense of inner steadiness. Try prioritizing blue-sky thinking, compiling and road testing your values, and identifying and refining your non-negotiables and measures of success.

When you are feeling worn out and running on empty, spend time *filling your tank.* This increases your stamina. Lighten your load and restore your energy in various ways. Some practices and tactics to try include determining where to spend your spoons, focusing on short-circuiting your suffering, and regularly releasing supposed career mistakes.

When you find yourself fixated on doing things right, the invitation is to practice *taking imperfect action.* This makes you nimble. Try engaging your intuition with the quick and dirty draft, focusing on getting to "good enough," and cultivating your curiosity with open-ended questions.

When you find yourself feeling thwarted and misunderstood or receive feedback that you are not being strategic enough, *fine tune your powers of observation*. Change from a narrow, transactional focus to see—and act on—the bigger picture. This results in insight into what is *truly* going on, both inside and around you. Some practices and tactics to try include reading the room, performing the Morning Scan, and calling on your future self.

If you are feeling isolated and alone, you are trying to do it all yourself. Turn your attention to *broadening your base of support* weaving a strong web of relationships with others. This increases your sense of stability. Some practices and tactics to try include setting your scaffolding for success, fostering strong relationships throughout the organization, and trying three things, three times, three ways.

If you feel like your points are not landing with your audience or you are not being seen as a compelling candidate for the opportunities you want, you are underinvesting in your assets. The opportunity is to increase your sense of self-confidence by *sharpening your professional narrative*. You can do this by reverse engineering what your target market wants, refining your elevator pitch and career headline, and shaping your accomplishments.

A SUCCESSFUL FORMULA FOR ANY CAREER MOVE

Following the strategies, practices, and tactics outlined in this book, you can distill what is important to you, examine options for closing the gap between where you are and where you want to be, and make progress in the direction of your choice. Once you have gained clarity around your non-negotiables, you have three potential paths forward:

1. Stay in the role or organization you are already in (assuming you are in one), transforming it from the inside out as best you can. This can be a short, medium, or long-term strategy.
2. Move to a new job in a new organization. This may include creating your own business or enterprise.
3. Pivot into a whole new career arena. This may require some training and an incubation period to establish.

By the way, it is possible to entertain more than one of these paths at once.

Hold multiple paths simultaneously

Tucker left for a several-month sabbatical after five years of service at his employer. During his tenure at an information security company, he had risen through the ranks to an executive role. Prior to leaving on sabbatical, his boss offered him a promotion. Tucker turned down the opportunity, sharing that he was considering a larger-scale change, and given his ambivalence it didn't feel right accepting. His boss encouraged him to take a break and then return to accept the promotion when he was feeling refreshed. Tucker accepted the proposal but resolved silently to explore potential new career directions during his time off. That's where I came in.

Tucker had wanted to start his own company for a long

time and had an idea in mind for a software application he could imagine a market for. Plus, he wondered if the grass was greener elsewhere and resolved to take recruiter calls to explore full-time roles with other employers. Since he had been honest about his desire for change, Tucker felt exploring various options during his break was an ethical thing to do. Navigating multiple potential paths at once made Tucker feel expansive and secure.

While gaining clarity on his non-negotiables, Tucker sketched out a rough vision for his startup. As he made progress outlining the key drivers of a satisfying career for himself, he also outlined the mission, vision, competitive landscape, product details, and possible business models for his fledgling enterprise. Once sufficiently clear on his entrepreneurial vision, he hired a small product design team to assemble a prototype of the application he was imagining. He rationalized that even if he decided to shelve the idea and come back to it later, there was value in capturing his idea visually.

Tucker also focused on refining how to describe the product and company to support eventual hiring and fundraising efforts. When not fleshing out his entrepreneurial venture, he conducted informational and networking conversations about full-time roles with companies that interested him, paying attention to where his energy was taking him and what he felt was his ultimate best fit.

Transform your current situation

Tucker's possible career directions included returning to his current employer in a similar role, but at a higher level.

When we began coaching, he was dead set against the idea. Over time he warmed to it as a viable option, especially when the economy faced a downturn. After outlining his startup idea, he turned his focus to what a return to his current employer would and could look like.

Out of the gate Tucker believed that if he returned to his full-time role, it would be impossible to start and run his own company. However, funding his own company to achieve market fit with the continued draw of a full-time salary was appealing, at least for the moment. Over time it became clear that one lever of influence Tucker had was to return to his job with strong boundaries on his time and leadership style, in order to reserve time and energy for his own enterprise. Doing so would make room for what really mattered to him: being entrepreneurial.

We examined how being entrepreneurial could take many forms, from launching his startup to sitting on boards or engaging as an angel investor. As part of his process, Tucker explored joining a venture capital firm in a full-time role to work with the firm's portfolio companies. This exploration solidified his desire to be an entrepreneur.

Returning to his current employer offered a lot of pros, provided he could reinvent himself there: his salary would stay the same or grow; he was respected for his knowledge and experience; he knew the organization inside and out; his employer was well-known in the industry; and his affiliation with the company brought prestige and credibility, making him a sought-after resource by industry organizations for speaking engagements and other professional opportunities. The trick would be to craft the role so that he could spend much of his time making a difference in the way he craved while minimizing what he did not like to do.

One area Tucker was particularly concerned about was his inability to say no to anyone asking for mentorship or time to help them further their career. His propensity to give away his precious time compromised Tucker's ability to ensure sufficient balance and downtime in his life. This signaled an area for possible optimization: streamlining the requests for his time into a more efficient delivery mechanism or establishing a set of downstream resources he could refer people to. These options had not occurred to him before, but with his non-negotiables in front of him, Tucker could see ways to reinvent himself with his current employer that he had not imagined before. This made that path feel both more energizing and viable, and was the route he ultimately took for a few months while he laid the groundwork for his fledging enterprise. Later, when he was ready, he made the jump full-time into his growing business.

PRACTICES AND TACTICS

Over thousands of coaching conversations, the thought and action patterns that keep professionals stuck have become crystal clear to me. A playbook has emerged from these findings, one that takes the form of strategies and tactics that include both a new way to *think* and to *be*. Here are some tactics to consider for your journey.

Start here

The seven traps we've discussed are the ones that, when you fall prey to them, cause the most damage to your career trajectory and well-being over time. They are also the ones that, when dealt with, allow your career to flourish in almost any situation. The good news is that you can travel from wherever you are now to where you want to be by addressing *your* gaps.

Suffering from one or more of the sabotaging mindsets and behavior patterns the seven traps represent is common and completely normal! We all fall prey to some or all of them. The good news is that unproductive approaches can be redirected to productive ones. This book has shown you how to do that.

After reading and reflecting on the stories and examples here, you may know which traps you most often get caught in. If you need help confirming the areas that most need your attention to increase your professional fulfillment, impact, and success, conduct a Self-Assessment. I've created a Self-Assessment Quiz and Results Key that you can access at **www.yourfinestwork.com**.

Whether or not you take the formal assessment, notice where your energy and attention goes. Are you sufficiently invested in all seven strategy areas? More embodied in some and less in others? Use your findings as a guide for how and where to best focus your attention and take action to build momentum toward your goals.

Take baby steps

"What I've learned is that it's a million little things, not the big things, that matter." Sadie, an advertising executive, was reflecting on her professional and personal development as we closed out the current phase of our work together.

She was referring to all the small tweaks in behavior and mindset she had made over the past few years to become more of the leader she wanted to be and more of what her team and organization needed from her.

It's the small steps, the tiny actions that get you to where you want to go, one bit at a time. Not sure where to start? The actions you take right now don't need to be big ones to have impact. Here are some ideas to consider:

To increase a sense of feeling grounded:

- Download a meditation app and begin a daily ritual of listening to one of the guided meditations. Try different options until you find one or two you like and then listen for as little as five to ten minutes a day to detach from your thoughts and ground yourself. You can even use them to help calm down at the end of the day and go to sleep!
- Restart a hobby you loved earlier in life but let fall by the wayside. Make an ironclad appointment with yourself to make time to pursue this love on a weekly basis.
- Identify a skill you love to use and offer it up to an organization or person who needs it.
- First thing in the morning, take out a blank page and start writing or drawing whatever comes to you at that moment. Checking your cell phone can wait for a few minutes.
- Find something you have been interested in learning and find a fun, engaging way to learn it—either reading a book, listening to a podcast, or taking a class.

To increase your satisfaction and visibility at work:

- Volunteer for a work project that allows you to gain visibility with senior leaders, even if it is outside your normal lane.
- Pick a skill that interests you and needs to be further developed to achieve your career goals. Take an online class in that area and make sure to engage with your leaders about what you are learning.
- Review your job duties and categorize which ones energize rather than drain you. Brainstorm ways to spend more time on the former and less on the latter; next, either delegate the draining work to others, systematize it to take less time and effort, or make the case to leadership to prioritize it off your plate.

To expand your professional platform and reach:

- Cultivate your voice by crafting articles, frameworks, or short videos that showcase your perspective in areas of functional expertise and interest. Either post these nuggets online to build visibility or curate them for your own purposes, building assets that you can use in various forms in the future, such as blog posts, book content, or speaking engagements.
- Update your resume and LinkedIn profile, highlighting what you want to be known for while speaking the language your target employer resonates with.

To indulge an entrepreneurial itch:

- Draft a rough cut of your vision for an entrepreneurial venture, noodling potential business models, competitive differentiation, and the value that the product or service will offer your target customer.
- Talk to people about your vision to gain feedback and refine your ideas further.
- Run some experiments to confirm your assumptions about your market and product or service viability with minimal investment. Step back to measure your results and see how you feel about continuing.

To strengthen your network:

- Actively seek out and grow one-on-one relationships with cross-functional peers and leaders, scheduling regular touchpoints to learn their key challenges and help them make progress against those objectives.
- Proactively upgrade the quality of your one-on-ones with your manager to transform them into strategic conversations. Set a strategic agenda that blends your career goals and your manager's objectives to create win-win outcomes.
- Reach out to former colleagues, classmates, and friends to reactivate and re-energize your professional network, providing support to those you care about but have lost touch with over the years.

I'm sure you get the idea. Honestly, it is more important to start moving in an energizing, positive direction than to make sure that the action you are taking is the "right" one. Just get into action, now. Don't wait until you have time or you figure out your life purpose or calling. Just find something that gives you joy, energy, and perhaps scares you just a bit to reach for and get started.

This is an unprecedented moment in time, a moment to wake up to the power you have over your life, to make your career what you want it to be and to make the impact you want in the world. Don't wait, because no one is going to do it for you, and it won't become easier to make time for it later. The people you admire, who inspire you by the way they live and work, are those who make tiny choices each day to bring more of what they want into their world, bit by bit, even when it scares them to do so.

Believe that you are worth taking the time each day to do something that energizes you, that lays down track for you to do more tomorrow and each day after that. You will be amazed at how things shift in your life when you spend moments each day taking small actions that add up to a big change over time.

Tackle multiple workstreams at once

Mark, a former caterer, had shut down his catering business, a fulfilling chapter in some ways but draining in others. For one, the long hours away from home were not conducive to his coveted role as a hands-on father. He loved to cook and felt committed to continuing to work with food but struggled to figure out the role and form that would take.

Though he wanted to be thoughtful in making his career transition, Mark bristled at the level of self-reflection and the slowing-down-to-speed-up it required.

When Mark found himself feeling impatient and wanting to get on with it, he followed a two-pronged strategy:

1. Recall his desire to be intentional with his next chapter and not just jump into something new.
2. Take action on practical tasks to feel a sense of forward progress.

This approach allowed him to muster the patience and reflection that conscious career design requires, while simultaneously taking action to make progress at a pretty good clip. Mark split his time, for example, between perusing business spaces available for rent for a possible restaurant, networking with people at cooking schools to understand what it would be like to work for one, and updating his resume and LinkedIn profile to solidify his professional narrative. Tackling these activities at the same time quelled his inner voice that was telling him he needed to get on with it already, while providing him information to refine his career direction.

Mark eventually decided to start his own lunch place, balancing his desires for hands-on cooking, directing a kitchen team, designing creative menus, relegating work to a single location, and holding boundaries with his schedule while allowing him to have adequate time with his family. This felt like an intentional move that he was excited to make.

If you, like Mark, want to keep an ongoing sense of

momentum-building, you can organize your time and effort into multiple channels of activity. These channels allow for progress on multiple fronts at once. For example, you can focus on one or more of the following channels of activity simultaneously to feel that sense of momentum building:

- listening to podcasts, reading articles and books on subjects related to your line of inquiry or interest
- researching companies you would want to work for, roles that could be a good match for your priorities or career arenas you may want to enter
- crafting your professional positioning to evolve the compelling story you tell yourself and others about the trajectory of where you've been in your career and where you are going
- fostering your network *inside* your organization to develop a strong web of resources to draw upon when you need it and to be seen as vital to those resources for the support you provide to them
- expanding your network *outside* your organization to have colleagues to draw upon when investigating new career chapters for yourself as well as best practices for your industry
- adjusting how you interact with your direct reports in meetings to try on different approaches to get the best from your team and to make sure they get the best from you

It is wise to clarify your non-negotiables first, as items build upon each other, and you will be most effective when drawing on that sense of internal steadiness.

YOUR BRIGHT FUTURE AWAITS

You have likely figured out by now that the journey to an ideal career is not a straight line but one full of twists and turns. Seemingly meandering yet deliberately focused, the journey requires a playbook to successfully navigate new and sometimes rugged terrain. This playbook guides you in your desired direction, regardless of whether you are growing in place or making a job or career change.

Career transformation comes from taking a series of baby steps that add up to a big shift over time. It's incredibly satisfying to move from feeling trapped in your position to negotiating intentionally for what you truly want and deserve. Identifying your desires and needs and then putting them out there so they can materialize for you is life-changing.

How exciting that you can access your finest work by concentrating on the seven strategies. When you do, you build a solid foundation under you and the ability to skillfully navigate your career to ever greater levels of fulfillment, impact, and success. With these tools in your toolbox, it truly is an exciting time to be alive.

You can start now to have more influence, impact, and fulfillment professionally. Doing so requires that you fully step into your potential and get out of your own way. You may feel an element of fear along with your ambition; that is completely normal!

However, you can dig deep and find the courage you need to take the journey toward more of what you want. Your experience will result in more satisfaction for you and a sense of connectedness with the larger collective consciousness rising in humanity to help us face the complex challenges of our time.

We need you to bring your best self to the world's challenges, to see how your personal journey to professional fulfillment is connected to the needs of the world. It is your privilege AND duty to pursue what is important to you. As a global community, we are facing challenges that are more complex than ever before, and our opportunity and mandate require us to bring the best of ourselves to face those challenges. Since we are all connected, the actions of one impact the outcomes of others. Rather than your pursuit of Livelyhood being a selfish one, it is the path to your greatest impact on yourself, your family, your employer, your local community, and by extension, humanity.

ACKNOWLEDGMENTS

I am fortunate in my work to be endlessly inspired by my clients. Many conversations over the years have yielded the rich stories that fill this book. I love what I do and appreciate that I have an insider's view of people's lives, walking alongside them as they transform their professional situations, one small action at a time. My clients know that I've been writing a book and have been my biggest advocates.

This book started with a promise my friend Debbie Devoe and I made to each other several years ago. Vowing to keep each other accountable with our respective writing projects, for several months we met each Tuesday morning at a local cafe to write. During those sessions, words poured out of me onto the page. Although I could not yet see how the ideas would come together into a cohesive message, I could tell even then that I had a message to share.

Soon after, I partnered with editor Kelley Sewell to formulate the book's early outline and shape the fundamental narrative. Kelley helped me believe in myself as a writer. Under her steady hand, the core manuscript came together.

Leeann Alameda, our marketing consultant, encouraged my writing through blogs and regular check-ins on how the book was coming. She introduced me to writer Casey McCabe, who helped refine my overall vision for the book as well as my definition of "Livelyhood."

Then I enrolled in a program to help emerging and

established writers publish their work. Raymond Aaron and his team guide participants through the publishing process. Through Raymond's program I was introduced to Tracy Knepple, a writer who helped me refine my voice.

Finally, I met Jon Harrison, the editor whose patient, thorough, and calming hand helped me to resolve the remaining structural issues in the narrative and to realize that what I have written is "good enough." Jon's contribution cannot be overstated. He helped me to streamline my ideas for clarity and simplify my language. He also imparted grammatical lessons I can apply to future writing projects.

When I ultimately decided to publish the book myself, Christine Keleny was a lifesaver and got me over the finish line.

David Houle, whom I admire greatly and draw inspiration and optimism from in my coaching and writing, kindly agreed to write the foreword. Coaches Laura Berman Fortgang and my A-List colleagues provided support and feedback as I refined the book's outline and ideas. I am grateful for the positive reinforcement my friend Christine Buck has consistently given me on my path to becoming a writer and to my friend Carisue Bench, who encouraged me to keep moving with this book.

Over the years I've drawn inspiration from the leaders I've met through the UCLA Anderson CEO Forum and Chief. My experiences in both organizations have informed both my coaching and my writing.

I appreciate the comradeship of the wonderful coaches and practitioners I've worked closely with over the years to service our clients, including Celia Stern, Deborah-Brown Volkman, Madelyn Mackie, Louise Goeckel, Lynn Landry, and Nancy Rothstein. Nancy took the headshot of me that graces the book's back cover and has supported me and our non-profit projects in the community.

During my years in product management, I had the good fortune to meet and work with Peter Weis. Later, when I decided to change careers, he gave me contract work during the transition and then was one of the first people to hire me as an executive coach to support his leaders.

My parents, Ron and Carol Clazie, have always believed in me; I am thankful for their constant support and unconditional love, as well as that of my brother, Ian. My husband Kevin is the backbone of my life, our family, and my coaching business. He keeps me grounded in my personal and professional endeavors. I appreciate his contributions to this book through feedback on the ideas as they have evolved, as well as the countless times he talked me down from the tree when I doubted myself and wondered if I would ever finish. Our children, Krista and Emmett, have helped their mom get out of her own way and just get on with it already. I am excited to watch them discover and create their own finest work.

I'm sure that I've left off some important people who have contributed meaningfully along my path to publish this book. To embrace my own concept of "good enough," I will close by saying that I am grateful to those who have held my hand along the way to becoming who I am. Your finest work has led me to mine. Thank you.

ABOUT THE AUTHOR

An ICF-certified master coach, Merideth shows executives how to look forward to Monday mornings. Since 2004 she has coached leaders to define their career priorities, assess the gap between those priorities and their current opportunities, and then close the gap to achieve fulfillment. Clients have grown their professional satisfaction, impact, and success, transforming their careers and leadership styles from the inside out.

Merideth coaches C-suite, senior and emerging leaders in service and product companies who have roles spanning technology, strategy, marketing and communications, operations, sales, and other strategic disciplines. She lives in the San Francisco Bay Area and coaches clients nationwide. Learn more about Merideth's work and access bonus materials for this book at **www.yourfinestwork.com**.